LOOKING INTO
THE EYES OF A KILLER
A Psychiatrist's Journey
through the Murderer's World

Drew Ross, M.D.

PLENUM TRADE • NEW YORK AND LONDON

Library of Congress Cataloging-in-Publication Data

On file

To life, the great teacher

ISBN 0-306-45791-1

© 1998 R. Andrew Schultz-Ross
Plenum Press is a Division of Plenum Publishing Corporation
233 Spring Street, New York, N.Y. 10013

http://www.plenum.com

Printed in the United States of America

Contents

Introduction   *7*

1. Staring into Ice   *17*

2. At the Crossroads of Healing and Punishment   *29*

3. Meeting the Murderer   *47*

4. Boredom behind the Headlines   *59*

5. The Thriller Killer   *69*

6. Beyond Insanity   *81*

7. The Sexuality of Violence   *89*

8. Late at Night   *99*

9. The Victim Is the Perpetrator   *107*

10. You Can Never Go Home   *119*

11. When the Plot Is the Illness   *127*

12. The Hole   *141*

13. The Mind Murderer   *149*

14. The Legal Criminal   *155*

15. Remorse   *161*

16. In the Face of My Own Fear   *173*

17. The Poetry of Insanity   *185*

18. Impossible Choices   *191*

19. The Child Child Murderer   *199*

20. In the Gang   *205*

21. Baby Death   *211*

22. The Doctor Voyeur and the Murderer
    Inside   *221*

23. Behind the Couch   *235*

24. A Crisis of Conscience   *243*

Acknowledgments   *259*

Index   *263*

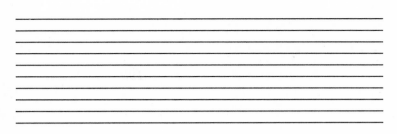

Introduction

THIS BOOK is about murder. Murder no longer surprises most readers. With countless television news and true crime books, one might imagine that everything has been said about it. Indeed, many of us worry about the increasing attention being paid to murder, especially with more and more graphic portrayals. Hasn't enough been said? My answer, and it almost surprises me, is no. While many words have been written, and perhaps more broadcast, I am not convinced that significant gains in meaning and understanding have occurred. Indeed, most coverage of the subject is not striving for meaning. Writers offer a portrayal of murder, perhaps in graphic detail, but often without meaningful context or interpretation.

There have been analyses and reanalyses of high-profile cases such as the bombing of the U.S. Federal Building in Oklahoma City and the murders for which O. J. Simpson was acquitted. Yet when I speak to people who have learned about these cases, they often seem lost in the details. Even the more deeply focused treatises on such cases seem to dwell more on how than why.

But such cases have attracted an enormous amount of attention. For Simpson, the issue of the spurned lover is probably not as fascinating as the idea of the fallen hero. He projected such an image of a clean-cut athlete that the idea of his having killed seemed incomprehensible to many. The fact that he was successful in a violent sport seems to be forgotten.

The bombing in Oklahoma City was a shock to Americans who thought that terrorism was unlikely to occur in the United States, and such shock was doubled by the fact that the terrorist was not foreign. The United States is a nation that feared an attack in World War II, and suffered essentially none on its shores after Pearl Harbor. Similarly, the cold war ended with some questions about the level of threat the Russians posed. To have a crushing blow dealt by an avowed patriot captured the attention of a citizenry already desensitized to mere murder. But I question whether any deep meanings have been found.

This book may not add meaning to murder either. Maybe murder is meaningless as well as senseless. But I hope that it will add a context, a description of some of the thinking patterns of those who plan or who are led into killing another person. This description, at least in realistic terms, is missing from most other books about murder. My book is not a theoretical treatise about violence, although my entrance into the world of murder was originally academic. I wanted to learn and study, as well as to treat. I had fully expected that a closer look at mentally ill murderers would bring some insight toward the development of a model or theory of violence that would help me and other students of behavior to understand. Such a theory would have to be published in the scholarly journals of my profession to be read and used by other professionals. Such journals publish well-researched, tidy work. Even in such an inexact science as psychiatry, the articles in medical journals are increasingly statistical. In other work, I attempted to gather such data. This book took me elsewhere. It took me on a highly personal journey into the minds of killers, within the confines of the confusing system that attempts to deal with them. Furthermore, the journey delved into the darker side of myself and others.

When I started work with murderers at the end of my training in psychiatry, most of my assumptions were soon challenged. Early on, I produced a simple working model of murder. It involved factors that might serve to either raise the level of drive toward violence or lower the inhibitions against it. Such factors include drug or alcohol use, social conflicts, or lack of support. Though far from earth-shattering, the model initially seemed to have value. Then, the edifice upon which it was built began to crack. Murder was not always the result of impulse. At times, it was intentional. I mean more than the legal "premeditation," which forms such a significant part of television courtroom arguments. The intention that I found in some murderers was deeper than the desire to harm another, or a fantasy about shooting an exlover. The intention that shocked me moved me away not from naiveté, but from denial. This powerful intention that I found in a few murderers was the lust for death. Somehow, I had hoped that murder was a result of anger gone awry, or a wish for the other to disappear. I had hoped that the conscious wish for death, the enjoyment of death, and the lust for another's death were all rare enough to be hard to find (except in fiction). They are not common but, unfortunately, not entirely rare either.

As I looked deeper, more fundamental assumptions were challenged. I came to this subject as a psychiatrist, trained to understand the mental illness of less violent individuals. Our understanding of mental health and illness involves theories that often work well to ease the ills of a depressed patient, for example. But our theories offer far less understanding of a murderer. Psychiatry, even many of the research aspects, is based upon the observation of clinical improvement. If something works, it forms the basis of a theory of causation. Both psychotherapy and medication work for depression; there are multiple theories of depression that relate the illness to conflicts amenable to therapy or chemical derangements responsive to drugs. But murder is usually not repeated. Once it has occurred, it cannot be undone. The idea of clinical improvement is elusive. Murderers seem to differ greatly from one another, as do the reasons for their acts. We have ideas and theories about violence, but they are preliminary and often sketchy. The legal system is troubled by psychiatry's shortcomings in explaining violence, as judges and attorneys would prefer more clear and crisp answers to questions about mental illness. They have a penchant for swift and absolute judgment: guilty or not guilty, insane or not, yea or nay. They assume the presence of such an answer. The reality is that there may be none, or it may be hard to find and more complex than yes or no. The legal system has little tolerance for relativity or uncertainty. Sometimes, the attorneys seem to latch on to the easy falsehood of an inexperienced or deceptive witness in order to avoid the discomfort of facing an uncertain truth. They want psychiatry to be more absolute, to give answers about the inner workings of the mind in clear, unequivocal terms. Indeed, despite our apprehensions (and equivocations), clear legal judgments are made.

This legal absolutism was no comfort for me, as I found examples of patients who clearly killed under the auspices of an unshakable and determinant psychosis, yet were placed in prisons where they were ill-afforded treatment. They were matched by others who had successfully bargained themselves into placement in hospitals where they did not belong. They accomplished this despite a decided lack of a clear psychiatric cause for the acts of homicide they had committed, only to find that getting released from a psychiatric hospital was probably harder than getting released from jail. The fact that there is no clearly defined release date for insanity acquittees is now being exploited by those who want sexual offenders in such hospitals to prevent their release. Some murderers seem unclassifiable as insane or not. There were ways in which they seemed ill, but they also seemed to have some control. Working on these difficult cases forced me to think about the ways that both the courts and psychiatrists viewed insanity.

The public often fears that the insanity defense means someone gets away with murder, but it may more realistically mean that hospitals are saddled with the responsibility for someone who doesn't fit. These cases led me to a number of questions. At first, the concept of insanity seemed fairly clear. Some people were too ill to be considered guilty of a crime that they committed. But then things began to get blurry. Was insanity more subtle or more complex than I originally had thought? Did the insanity defense really help the unfortunate few driven into action by illness, or had the intent of the law been lost?

These debates led me to try to understand the differences between psychiatry and the law. Why did psychiatrists and lawyers sometimes seem to think so differently?

Through my training and career, I tried to understand the roots of these differences. There were differences in theory, in the manner that each understood the causes and effects of behavior. At first, the differences seemed subtle. Later they were clear, and then stark. Lawyers look for motive, a clear external goal for behavior, whereas psychiatrists tend to look for internal motivation, whether emotional or chemical. Lawyers fit behavior into criminal classifications that roughly measure the severity of a crime. Psychiatrists use classifications of diagnosis that group patients based on patterns of symptoms more than severity. Lawyers look to the statutes and a rich tradition of past cases in order to find trends and judgments. Psychiatrists have textbooks but few if any "laws" that scientifically explain behavior, but can look to a long tradition of observations and, more recently, experiments. Lawyers take one side

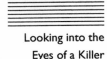
or the other, based on who their client is, but a psychiatrist's moral obligation as an evaluator is to the truth and, as a treating physician, to the patient.

I found that looking closely at theory—the way psychiatrists and lawyers think—helped me understand a great deal. But there was more. Though I still struggle with the limitations of the theories of psychiatry and the law, I began to realize that this book would have to reach beyond them. My work had begun to reach deeper within me than theory. Forced to abandon my crutches of educated knowledge, I began to question society's near-sacred assumption that murder is inhuman. Day after day, I found tragic, cruel, or even pedestrian reasons and explanations for murder, but they were all chillingly human. Thus, though my bearing and conduct in my duties remained professional, my understanding of violence became personal. Confronted with humanity inside the walls of a prison, I looked inside myself to find the reasons I had been drawn there, as I slowly grew to understand the men and women around me.

This book represents this journey into the world of murderers through my work as a forensic psychiatrist. In this capacity, I have examined many murderers in order to try to reach some academic understanding of violence, to prepare reports for the legal system, and to provide clinical treatment. In doing so, I found that I could not remain detached from and unmoved by what I saw. I found myself confronted with violence not as an abstract concept, but as an often recent event in the life of a living, breathing human being sitting across the table from me. I found myself on a journey into the world and the mind of the killer.

Yes, I was scared. But not only scared. Learning about murder caused me to learn about my own assumptions and those of the civilization that we contrive to represent when we attempt to interact with those who have violated the most sacred taboo and killed another human being. Working with murderers caused me to be that civilization's representative in court and in the murderer's world. That led me to realize that the medical and legal systems contained problems that seemed to deepen as I looked further.

The information in this book results not only from the public court record, but also from professional interactions that I would prefer remain confidential. Also, because many murders are unusual and recognizable, I have had to change identifying details. However, I tried always to keep the stories true to form. It is this form, or meaning, behind murder that is the subject of this book. The balancing act of maintaining both unrecognizability and realistic portrayal was difficult but possible because of the significant overlap of many murderers' lives when viewed at the "form" level. This statement is not meant to imply that murderers are homogeneous. Rather, the core dramas for all of us, nonmurderers included, usually center on a limited number of critical events: love, loss, loneliness, striving, success, failure, creation, and demise. It is at this core level of experience, a level that we share with prisoners and idols alike, that murder becomes more understandable. By maintaining truth at this level, all of the layers of details can be safely altered.

I have been especially sensitive to the potential perceptions of the patients and inmates who have interacted with me, and who may search for their individual stories herein. They will be successful in only the most global sense.

In maintaining this level of confidentiality, I have closely adhered to standards articulated for the purpose of scientific literature. However, I have written in a more confidential manner than recommended in these guidelines because of my intended lay audience.

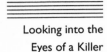

My efforts at devising a means of maintaining confidentiality while assuring thematic accuracy have forced me to sharpen the thinking in this book far more than if I had told the stories straight out. This additional work, I believe, has led me to a deeper understanding than I felt at the beginning of this enterprise. I hope that it is adequately reflected herein.

People read about murder because the subject is exciting. Fair enough, but my intent is also to challenge the reader. Some of the most popular books and films on this topic contain a number of facile assumptions that I dispute. While I have no argument with a quickened pulse, I hope that it is accompanied by an open mind.

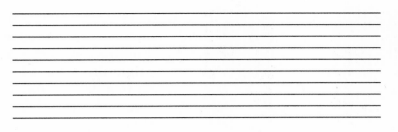

1

Staring into Ice

I WAS TIRED on the day that I met Gary. I had been working hard at two jobs and I was irritable, if not downright angry, when he was interviewed. He was tall, and he entered the room with a faintly coy amble. His piercing eyes never seemed to waver. These eyes immediately caught my attention, because they told a different story than his apparent sense of ease. On closer examination, there were more signs that he was tense and angry. His jaw was clenched, and his face never smiled or frowned. Each movement was made with taut muscular action, as if even walking were an aggressive act. The cocky, casual air that he superimposed on this tension was a thin and frail layer indeed. Even a seemingly casual conversation was met with his silent, searching hostility. His eyes told more than his muscular tension or curt, exasperated sighs when a question was asked that he didn't like. The cold anger became steel. I repeatedly raised my head above my notes and caught those stern eyes that fluidly tracked my every motion and, it would seem, intention. All the while, his calculated, vague answers portrayed a sense of benign ignorance, while his eyes told of penetrating knowledge. My mind drifted from the substance of the evaluation. I struggled for the right word to describe his eyes. There was something militaristic, but they were not filled with the dogma of old soldiers. They were ready for attack. There was a laser-like quality; the eyes had an eerie electric blueness and smooth, mechanical pursuit. It was finally the hunter that I saw in those eyes, the faraway eagle or condor sighting prey

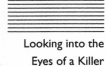
in their ignorance and, with the same smooth but tense motion, moving in closer for the inevitable conclusion. The eyes, and the man, were predatory.

Gary came from a hard family in a tough section of a major city. His father was not a serious criminal, but was an alcoholic whose children were a relatively unwanted interruption in a life of drugs and debauchery. Perhaps the only way that Gary garnered attention from his father was to commit crimes. At times, his father was violent and angry toward Gary, but in the early days, he was amused and even excited by Gary's antics. Gary's mother had little to do with him for weeks at a time, but when he got into trouble, she would rush to his defense. As Gary got older, he wooed women who treated him in a pattern similar to his mother's. Each would tell him to stay out of trouble, but would become loudly supportive when he was arrested. Perhaps he was aided by this disturbing, but common type of support in which only misbehavior gets rewarded by attention. For whatever reasons, Gary escalated from minor troublemaking as a child to major burglary as an adult.

He was handsome, and when one woman would tire of him (often during his brief previous jail sentences), he would soon find another. At a certain level, he felt impregnable. He usually had companionship, a flashy car, and plenty of excitement. It may have been the latter that really maintained Gary's criminality. On close inspection, there were at least a few clues to understand his emotions and the roles of the people around him. His relationship with his parents seemed to revolve around his arrests. They would avoid talking about his problems. As he aged and his sentences in prison lengthened, they pulled away without explanation. Each time he was arrested, they would help, but with growing resignation and lessening excitement. Even this form of attention seeking was drying up.

No girlfriend was brave or foolish enough to confront him, either. He would break up with a woman if
he thought that she was beginning to understand him
or outsmart him. He picked out a woman to pursue if
his friends thought she was attractive. Even sex was
brief and emotionally shallow, a conquest to brag about.
He did not feel any understanding for sex besides tension relief and another "score."

Movies were a major source of both sexual and
personal identities. If a man in a movie seemed smooth
or capable, Gary, especially in his younger days, would
watch the movie two or three times to "get down the
moves." He would learn how to toss his head, how to
walk, how to act tough.

On his last break-in, the owner of the home ran to
use the phone to call the police. Gary strangled her and
attempted to make it appear that she had committed
suicide. He said, "She did commit suicide, by ever
messing with me. Don't talk your justice with me. I
have my own justice." When a social worker attempted
to interview Gary, he told him, "Get lost. I don't need
you people. The only thing wrong with me is you guys."
Gary's presentation was always the same. He was not
always overtly angry, but he was always absolutely
cold, and he never showed any remorse. He explained
his violence by claiming that it was a result of his drug
use. He said something like, "Drugs are an illness,
right? That's what they all say, A.A. [Alcoholics Anony-
mous], N.A. [Narcotics Anonymous], the drug counselors, everybody. And when you're using, it's like they
have the control. The drugs take over and do it all. People like even didn't recognize me when I was using
heavy. You look different, you don't shave or nothing,
clothes or appearance doesn't matter, just drugs. So,
you become like an animal, starving for drugs. It is
all the drugs, always the drugs that got me into trouble. People told me to stay away from them, but I was

hooked, I was addicted. The counselors say that some people can take a drink now and then, no problem, maybe even drugs. But an alcoholic thinks he can, like I did, but he can't. I used to think that I could control it, but I learned that it controls me. So now, I'm clean, real clean, all the meetings and all, so I'm okay now, I'm fine. Clean and sober." In this way, he tried to explain away his past acts and minimize his potential for danger in the future.

To sit with him was to sit with fear, because his attractive face and carefully casual haircut did not hide the danger. He did not have the indifferent disregard of an angry teenager. Instead, he had a constant vigilance that may have been the source of my identification of him as a predator. There was always a sense of imminence, that he was preparing to pounce. Perhaps only the unsuspecting were in danger from him. In prison, the inmates size each other up and create a pecking order of minor to major abuse. No one bothered Gary.

In a situation where the danger was removed, where the chilling fear could subside, to sit with Gary was to sit alone. Beyond the anger, there was nothing. He would sit, trying to instill fear, and failing that, anger. I found myself wondering if that really was all there was. I wondered if Gary could only see himself in the fear, rejection, and anger that he brought out in others. When it failed, he would sit, faintly sad, like a pouting, mischievous boy in the principal's office. At that moment, he would arouse a faint sense of empathy for the emptiness.

Gary's presence's in this book is not surprising. Indeed, one of the difficulties in understanding murder is that many people assume that his is the only type of murderer. Gary is a cold-blooded killer. He is antisocial, or what some describe as a sociopath or, for drama, a psychopath. These are terms, roughly synonymous, for individuals who are repetitive criminals with little regard for other people or for their dignity. They are able to cunningly plot and ruthlessly enact a murder, and smile about it. In this sense, they appear to be like many television villains, upset only if they are caught. Yet, there are some subtleties even for this type of killer who seems to conform to our expectations (to a frightening degree).

Allan, for example, seemed different from Gary. Allan was thirty years old when he was convicted. He was attractive, but in a less "bad boy" style than Gary. He had neatly combed black hair and an engaging, business-like smile. He emphasized points in conversation by leaning closer to the interviewer. When asked about his childhood, Allan said, at first, that it was "uneventful, suburban, probably like most upper-middle-class people." When encouraged to continue, he said that his mother was "quiet, and deep down, nice, I guess. I really didn't talk to her much. Dad was the boss, but ineffectual really, I had to take the risks for him." Actually, his father was moderately successful in business but lost money in gambling. Allan stole money from his father's business, and at first, also gambled and lost. He said, "Just like Dad, I was no good at the horses," with a smile. Eventually, he "invested" his father's money in a business selling drugs that became highly profitable. His partner, who helped him get started, was murdered. At first, Allan said, "I didn't have nothing to do with it." He wore a prison-issued sweatshirt, but he cut the sleeves off. Sitting sideways in the chair, with his arm draped over the back, he had the demeanor of a young patrician at the athletic club. He smiled and chatted about his case as if it happened to someone else. "Some of the guys in the organization knew he had betrayed us, and they went after him. I couldn't stop them. I didn't know." Later, he conceded that "drugs is a rough business. You sign your own death warrant if you betray someone. My partner knew he was history. He was lucky that I didn't kill him myself. I would have done it right. He was scum." Moments after this discussion, he was smiling and engaging again. He said, "Doctor, I was really hoping that you could help me out with this case because I'm looking at some serious time here, but it wasn't like the way they're trying to make it look. They're trying to make it like this big mob hit thing. They're trying to make me out to be some guy who should spend the rest of his life away because I'm so bad. I'm not a bad guy, huh, Doc? I've been okay with you, right? You treat me straight, I'll treat you straight. This guy wasn't no victim. He was way out there, way out over the line. They said this thing in the paper about his poor wife and kids, but, man, the guy was out there cheating on her right and left, and he was screwing up the business real bad, too." Allan was convicted of conspiring to have his partner killed. By his account, he had been handed a "raw deal."

When not directly challenged about his case, Allan would smile engagingly. Upon entering a room, he would visually or verbally greet all. He was often politely complimentary, saying, "Nice tie" or "Did you have your hair cut?" In short, he could be charming. After knowing Allan for a year or more, it became easier for me to see the differences between his pleasantries and those exhibited normally in the office or at a social gathering. I could almost hear the gears moving in Allan's head, because each of his actions was a calculated mechanical exercise for a designated purpose. When he thought that I might be able to shorten his stay, he was not only pleasant with me, but he also convincingly displayed concern about his past issues and inquired thoughtfully about the status of an ill staff member. However, when surreptitiously observed with other inmates, he was bossy, brazen, and mean. Over time, his attempts at emotional bribery began to make me feel like I did upon the receipt of a flowery, preprinted greeting card overflowing with generic, stale emotion. Nonetheless, in short interactions with staff who did not know him, his attempts were often successful.

Sociopaths are masters at faking emotion, even remorse. This ability creates one of the most difficult challenges of work with criminals, separating the sociopathic fake from the genuine article. Sociopaths are notoriously skilled at faking well, and the more skilled the sociopath, the less sociopathic he (or, less commonly, she) appears to be. The seemingly genuinely remorseful murderer is either truly remorseful or a highly skilled sociopath.

This skill does have another side. Sociopaths are often assumed to be somehow disconnected from human emotions. This assumption seems reasonable given the level of lack of remorse seen, for example, in Gary. Yet, Allan shows us that the sociopath can read others' emotions very well, and, at the least, can seem to have the emotion he thinks will benefit him in the interaction. In this sense, the sociopath is connected to other people and to human emotion through his observation of others and imitation of emotion to achieve his ends. While this connection is based on a fundamental level of falsehood, it may be the closest connection the sociopath can muster.

Indeed, the sociopath is likely to be angry when his lies are discovered. Certainly, most of his disappointment lies in not getting what he wants. But, he also loses the human connection. Although it is based on a lie, it may be the only one he has.

Successive disappointments can eventually lead to some degree of change. Lester was very similar to Allan when he was younger, although he was less wealthy and more wild. He rode around town on a loud Harley-Davidson motorcycle with no helmet, whistling at women and cursing at men. He drank often, and lost

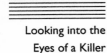

a series of house-painting and auto-repair jobs due to drunkenness, or more often, uncouth behavior toward the boss. He served a short sentence for burglary and had a prior probation for receiving stolen merchandise. He was treated for substance abuse twice, once through the prison program and subsequently at the strong urging of his family. He was frequently in fights and had seriously hurt some of his opponents. Although handsome as a younger man, as he advanced through his thirties, the combination of cigarettes, poor nutrition, and alcohol took its toll. His face began to seem drawn. He later sprouted a belly that didn't match his lanky gait. After the last of a series of violent disputes with his girlfriend, she left him. Having maintained a painting job for some time, he bought a new motorcycle, perhaps as a diversion from the loss of his girlfriend. After drinking, he rode to his sister's house. They drank more together. Lester asked his sister to take a ride with him. Lester drove, and his sister climbed on the motorcycle behind him. Speeding around a corner, Lester lost control. The big motorcycle hurled them toward the embankment on the side of the road. Lester escaped with a broken arm, but his sister was killed instantly. His version of the story was, "I didn't have to go nowhere special that day. I was just real proud of that new Harley. She was real shiny and nice and I was showing her off to everybody. Back when I was younger, my sister used to like to ride. She dated a biker for a while one time, but she ain't been on one for a long time. So, I'd thought I'd take her for a ride. Wasn't going nowhere in particular." When I asked him about the amount of alcohol, he smiled with a touch of embarrassment. "It wasn't that much, really. I've drunk a lot more and drove fine." When I pressed him, he admitted that he had consumed several six-packs of beer. "But that wasn't it, really. I drive good when I'm drunk. There had to be something there. There must have been something, some car out of control or a patch of oil." He was so drunk at the time that he didn't remember the accident. Despite his attempts to explain what happened, he felt guilty about his sister's death.

His family was understandably angry. While he tried hard to rationalize the death as being due to some unrecalled event, the overwhelming impact of the loss of his youth, his girlfriend, and his sister led to the beginning traces of insight about the degree to which these losses hinged on his own behavior. In the past, the blame was always directed elsewhere, a process simply and accurately termed *externalization*. Prison sentences were blamed on the judge, jury, or inadequate counsel. He blamed his violence on the victim who provoked him, or as Lester put it, "set him off." Perhaps the strongest impetus to insight, however, was Lester's son. He had started to get into trouble for his difficulties with alcohol and stealing. At first, Lester thought that his son's minor troublemaking was entertaining. But as the level of misbehavior worsened and the consequences increased, Lester became annoyed. It was disturbing to have to pick someone else up at the police station. Lester's son also externalized the blame for his misdeeds, and Lester could see that process in his son before he could notice it in himself. However, as his own life began to unravel, it hurt more to see his son following in his footsteps. Although I could not forgive him for his many acts of violence and the reckless death of his sister, I had a faint sense of hope and encouragement for his bravery in beginning to look at himself. Many sociopaths end up dead or in prison. Some surprise us by improving. Unfortunately, it is often only after ruining or ending others' lives.

2

At the Crossroads of Healing and Punishment

I'T'S AN UNLIKELY place for a correctional facility. There's a wooden sign at the entrance to the road. The sign has too many words to read on it while moving; at a glance, it looks like the sign for a national park, with all of the rules. A smaller sign reads, "Private road, Use at own risk." After a short run of woods, the road opens up to a large field. A huge prison, surrounded by shiny fences looped at the top with coils of barbed wire, stands in the distance. Two more buildings are farther away; again, there are the fences, again, the barbed wire. Along the road, there are dark Ford sedans with stars on the side. Eyes peer out of them. You are watched as you pass. Over the hill, the road dead-ends into a set of low buildings surrounded by two parallel fences topped with wire. On closer inspection, it is a sharper, flatter variant of barbed wire appropriately known as razor wire. As night falls, the loops pick up the bright lights and glow, sharp points and round loops gleaming.

This is a hospital.

A few years ago, an old friend asked me what I did for a living. I said, "Forensic psychiatry." His nose twisted as he pondered it. Forensic, he thought, as in the television show *Quincy,* as in dead people. Psychiatry, as in Freud, the couch, and dreams. As he reached this impossible juxtaposition, I said, "Yeah, I do therapy with dead people."

I have thought about this joke many times because it contains two themes of vital concern to a forensic

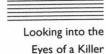
psychiatrist: impossible juxtaposition and familiarity, if not flippancy, with horror.

Forensic psychiatrists evaluate and treat criminals with mental illness. The historical term, *criminally insane,* is still used occasionally, mainly in horror movies. This patient population is both dangerous and difficult. These patients often have a blurry combination of drug abuse, neurologic illness, psychiatric illness, and bad luck. This mixture of problems means that the patients are difficult to treat; their problems are as far from the "clean" disorders found in the textbooks as the prison is from a suburban clinic. Doctors who treat these people take different approaches. Some ignore the suffering and call the patients liars, since they often try to manipulate the system. Other doctors take on their cause, rebelling against the authorities, and perhaps ignoring some of the prisoners' cruelty to themselves and others.

The psychiatrists who evaluate criminals face no less of a challenge. They have to tell the court what to make of these difficult people. Generally speaking, the roles of evaluator and treater are better kept separate. That separation allows the treater to try to ally with the patient and the evaluator to tell what may be the rather unkind truth. Many forensic psychiatrists treat some individuals and evaluate others. Much of the difficulty in the evaluation process is the complexity of the patients. The real challenge, however, may be the wooing of two strange bedfellows, law and psychiatry.

If the law were a person, and a mentally ill person, he or she might have borderline personality disorder, the controversial diagnosis perhaps portrayed in the film *Fatal Attraction.* Patients with this disorder have difficulty maintaining either a sense of self or maintaining relationships. They are frequently self-destructive. Most important for this example, they often have a notoriously all yes-or-no way of looking at things. The school of cognitive psychotherapy has focused on the emotional consequences of patterns of thinking. They have defined this pattern as black-and-white thinking, and have noticed that it can lead to false, simple conclusions. A child of a technological age, I prefer to call it binary logic. Whatever it is termed, the law has it. You are either guilty or not guilty; it is either in the statutes or not. You may appeal a decision, and the courts might reverse it (psychoanalysts call that *doing and undoing*), but the courts will almost never say maybe.

Psychiatry, on the other hand, is notoriously ambivalent. It tolerates the coexistence of mutually exclusive ideas better than any discipline I know, excepting perhaps philosophy and, of course, politics. Perhaps most famously, psychiatry contains within it the teachings of Freud, a man who has been labeled as both the brilliant discoverer of the unconscious and a sexist. He certainly was no feminist, but it might be far-fetched to demand a man of the Victorian age to have anticipated the social trends that followed him. Yet all of psychiatry is not Freudian. It also contains the work of the mystical Jung, the rigid Skinner, and a cavalcade of brain biologists. While law arguably has as many factions, case by case, someone makes a judgment. Psychiatry remains divided, or, as we like to say, eclectic. Forensic psychiatry has often been criticized for its ability to pull forth two experts who will present two seemingly opposite conclusions about the same case.

The differences between law and psychiatry extend deeper and find their roots in the history of these two disciplines. Psychiatry and the law each have many roots, but I will try to trace those that I find to apply in their meeting.

The law is deeply rooted in Greek and Roman thinking, melted together with subsequent religious ideas on morality. Plato wrote that the law was based on the supposition that both sides were at war; perhaps the adversarial nature of the proceedings runs very deep. American law is predominantly based on English common law. Both assume, as some of the ancient Greeks did, that the truth comes out if there are strong opposing forces and a righteous battle. It has been my experience that many Asian and Polynesian people and lands that are accustomed to patterns of settling differences with greater degrees of consensus and accommodation often have great difficulty if they are forced to adjust to this system and to the righteous battle as the model for legal matters (even wars have been fought differently). The English are also a culture that has historically placed great emphasis on the differences between the nobility and the commoners. This tradition is reflected in the discourse between the attorneys and judge. Ironically, the proceedings are recorded as if the defendant presented the case, "Smith argued . . . ," but even rather intelligent psychiatric patients are usually quite in the dark as to the full meaning of the words and jockeying that takes place. Justice as a virtue seems more related to intellectual matters—how well the game is played, how referenced the proceedings are to past judgments. Again, such justice may literally be at the level of the judge, but results in strange consequences when viewed at the level of the defendant.

For example, in one jurisdiction, there is a remarkable difference between the two major methods of hospitalizing patients with mental illness. Most, if not all, jurisdictions have both. The first is a civil commitment process to hospitalize patients against their stated will if they are quite ill. Civil commitment exists because it is recognized that some patients may need treatment and not realize it. It is often the family or treating clinicians that petition the court for an involuntary hospitalization. The second method is a process to hospitalize patients charged with a crime. In many jurisdictions, the two statutes are similar or even linked. But, in at least one state, the statutes are amazingly different. There, a patient must be both ill and imminently dangerous to be placed in the hospital by the civil proceeding. Proving that danger is imminent is difficult; many patients who are quite ill have difficulty taking care of themselves but do not appear to be in imminent danger. Yet if that same patient commits a minor criminal offense such as stealing food, he or she can be committed by the criminal proceeding to the same hospital by virtue of the presence of the illness alone. The illness must be of the severity that it might impair his or her abilities at trial, but there is a vast difference in difficulty here—danger that looks immediate versus the mere presence of illness. Many patients ill enough to need to be hospitalized have disorganized behavior that could lead to either a civil or criminal proceeding. Yet because of the vast difference in the laws, the outcome for the same person could be different, and there is a tendency for patients to be arrested, since it may afford them treatment. At the judge's level, we can understand that the two arenas of law have different traditions, and that the law sees confinement of a noncriminal differently than that of a criminal. But the patient sees absurdity.

Psychiatry, at some level, started before we declared the separation of mind and body. Ancient wisdom, especially in Asia, linked mental ills to difficulties in spiritual development and found links between physical and environmental causes. Traditional Chinese medicine is finding greater acceptance in the West, at least in terms of the use of acupuncture. But the idea that anger, love, and other emotions are as much physical as mental is only accepted in a rudimentary sense. Many of us hope for a reunion of the physical, emotional, and spiritual issues in psychiatry that were separated in the mainstream of the profession long ago. Psychiatry, like other sciences, began to doubt the existence of unseen forces and tried to find truth in the measurable and observable. The idea that deeper meanings might be present but elusive to the senses is perhaps again gaining ground, but research in such arenas is limited by the nearly religious adherence to empiricism in Western science.

Physics may have been the most extreme of these sciences, perhaps the scientific king of observable phenomena. Yet, with quantum physics, this science was forced to face the reality of unseen and difficult-to-measure forces. Relativity further banished the idea of measuring a truth that is completely separate from the observer and objectively true. Remarkably, the social and natural sciences have just begun really to incorporate these ideas.

Psychiatry has had an interesting relationship with the issue of unseen forces. Early mystical ideas revolved around such forces. The Renaissance is better known for the resurgence of the arts, but it also involved a greater focus on the power of humans as opposed to deities. There was a great interest in mechanical objects and a movement toward the observation of measurable phenomena that affected the psychology of the day. Later, about one hundred years ago, Emil Kraepelin made some of the most memorable observations by detailing the symptoms and usual course of the illnesses that we now call schizophrenia and bipolar disorder (manic–depressive illness). Kraepelin is often revered by the champions of the measurable. He was, at least in the United States, somewhat forgotten as Freudian psychiatry burgeoned and then declined.

Freud learned much from thinkers that preceded him, including Pierre Janet. Janet was interested in, and may have "discovered," the unconscious before Freud. Janet certainly was interested in hypnosis and unseen causation, but Freud made the concept of the unconscious famous. Some have argued that Freud contributed little, or at least was not a revolutionary thinker, but that argument may really relate to the fact that most scientific discoveries only appear to come out of "nowhere." When the course of events is carefully traced, apparently revolutionary discoveries often turn out to be a series of small steps taken by various researchers. Perhaps less commonly, radical shifts and more unexpected discoveries also occur. The unconscious is now practically synonymous with psychic unseen causation, so it is not surprising that some view Freud's work as a step against science. That view is only true if science is limited to purely seen forces.

The impossible juxtaposition of psychiatry and the law presents a series of derivative, equally impossible juxtapositions. One of my duties early in my work with violent people was to decide whether a given patient needed to stay at the forensic hospital beyond a brief period of evaluation. Most people wouldn't want to stay there, but you might, if you were in prison.

The first criterion that we used in this decision was daunting enough. Did the patient have a mental illness? Although this question is easy when someone is very ill, most criminal defendants have had difficult lives, car accidents, and drug problems. On close examination, there often was evidence of impairments in thinking, reasoning, and responses to emotions. Whether these impairments rose to the level of illness for the sake of the evaluation was usually a judgment call.

The second criterion was difficult to understand in the light of a more retributive national policy in the field of corrections. Was the person psychologically able to serve in a penal environment? Although I did not dwell on the issue at the time, this question bothered me. Was a psychologically well person better able to receive punishment? I was never sure if anyone really was. The third criterion bordered on the absurd. Was the patient dangerous if not kept at the hospital? This

question is difficult; violence is often an eruptive, passionate event. The question is not made simpler by the
further stipulation that the danger was supposed to
be due to mental illness. This distinction is a tough
one; it demanded discerning whether a given person's
danger resulted from his or her choices, or was caused
by an illness. Figuring out causation proved to be very
difficult.

As I noted earlier, some patients were clearly ill.
Yet their criminality and danger didn't always disappear with treatment of the illness. We can treat mental
illness, but when the illness is improved and the criminal behavior isn't, we generally have little to offer. In
this situation, psychiatry hasn't figured out what to do.

The public hasn't decided what it wants to do with
criminals either. Many are critical of psychiatrists' involvement with the insanity defense, which involves a
different and probably more difficult psychiatric evaluation. The role of the expert witness in insanity defenses captures the most media attention in forensic
psychiatry. The first historical record of essentially
psychiatric testimony (the term *psychiatrist* is more recent) was in Britain in 1760. Earl Ferrers had shot his
steward and killed him. By virtue of the law of the day,
he conducted his own defense and tried to prove that
he was insane, with the help of testimony from Dr.
John Monro, who was the physician superintendent of
Bethlem, the place that is literally known as Bedlam.
History records that the high quality of the Earl's defense backfired; it was difficult to believe that a man
was insane if he was skilled at presenting legal matters in court.

The modern era in conceptualizing criminal insanity began after Britain tightened up the use of the defense in response to attacks on key leaders during
Queen Victoria's reign. Edward Oxford attempted to
assassinate Queen Victoria in 1840; he was acquitted

by reason of insanity. Then, Daniel M'Naghten mistook Edward Drummond, personal secretary to Sir Robert Peel to be Peel, then the prime minister. M'Naghten killed Drummond and was acquitted after the testimony of nine experts. After the acquittal, the Queen and the nation were upset; the judges subsequently revised the rules for insanity; the M'Naghten rule cites that "to establish a defense on the ground of insanity, it must be clearly proved that at the time of the committing of the act, the party accused was labouring under such defect of reason, from disease of the mind, as not to know the nature and quality of the act he was doing, or if he did know it, that he did not know he was doing what was wrong." This standard is still used in parts of the United States and is perhaps the basis of most of the other standards. It was criticized for not including the possibility that a person with psychosis might know about his or her act, and even that it was wrong, but not be able to reasonably apply this knowledge. Many newer standards are softer on the quality of the knowledge and include psychotic effects on behavior, since it is widely believed that an ill person may act oddly even when there is a preservation of knowledge that the behavior is considered to be wrong. In a turn of events recalling M'Naghten, John Hinckley's attempt on the life of Ronald Reagan and his subsequent acquittal by reason of insanity was followed by a tightening of the federal standard for insanity. This change eliminated the part that allowed psychotically based behavior and kept only derangements of knowledge as the standard for insanity. This standard affects only federal crimes; each state sets its own standard.

The insanity defense shines stark, bright lighting on the impossible juxtaposition of law and psychiatry. In court, there is usually a psychiatrist who views the case from a perspective that gives insanity a narrow, legal definition. It is often difficult to reconstruct the emotional state of a person at the time of a crime, and more conservative physicians are wary of the patient who may fake illness. Also, many patients have been medicated prior to trial and appear much less ill on examination than they may have been in the fateful instant of the crime. It is sometimes hard to really fathom the depths of an illness when the patient appears much better after being treated.

Of course, there are other psychiatrists who go to the opposite extreme and seem to think that any mental illness should bar or limit culpability. They sometimes offer a very forgiving opinion that links crime (abnormal behavior) with mental illness (patterns or syndromes of abnormal behavior). Indeed, most criminals have had difficult lives. The thorough search of a criminal's history is likely to reveal traces of evidence of psychological difficulty. It is clear, however, that not all criminals are seriously mentally ill. The presentation of alternative views of illness to the jury is probably valuable, but the apparent contradiction of two well-spoken expert witnesses giving opposing views tends to make psychiatry seem too pliable. The presence of "hired gun" forensic experts who give the opinion they are being paid to give is a regrettable blight upon the profession.

Clearly, more knowledge is needed. Forensic psychiatry is a relatively young subspecialty, and research and theoretical inquiry are slowly growing. The absurdity of the marriage of law and psychiatry may prove to be a backhanded boon to research. I have noticed that I have a much keener sense of the tacit assumptions of psychiatry from looking at it within a legal framework. Similarly, legal colleagues have noted that they have learned much about the quirks of the law by putting themselves in the shoes of psychiatrists.

Many people accuse psychiatrists of having a high rate of mental illness. While I doubt that our rate of ill-

ness is much higher than other professionals and
physicians, I think and hope that our level of curiosity
and reflection on our own psychological issues is higher.
We often try to understand ourselves through our understanding of others. But it can be a mistake to apply
this paradigm in reverse. You cannot expect that others
do things for the reasons you would. Criminal offenders test the limits of our empathy. They are often very
different people than most psychiatrists or attorneys,
with different backgrounds, ideas, and motivation. The
attempt to understand their motivation stretches the
skills of both the lawyer and psychiatrist.

Part of the difficulty with the insanity defense,
and in work with sociopaths, is that neither mental illness nor criminality is a crisply demarcated concept.
What if a man steals a car because he believes that all
of the riches of the world are his due because of a delusional degree of grandiosity? Or if a woman hears a
voice that says that her town is a bad place to live, and
she steals a car because it offers a comfortable and
convenient means of exit? Such "split hair" decisions
may be more common than cases in which the illness
clearly led to the criminal activity. Part of the difficulty
is that the central issue in these decisions is a professional opinion about the legal issue of responsibility.
Having an illness is not enough; one has to get into the
thick of the relationship of the symptoms to the crime.

Most people don't think criminal behavior has biological causes. Watching a man steal someone's purse
doesn't usually lead to a concern that there is a chemical problem in his brain. But this commonsense notion,
shared by many professionals, could serve as a block to
the exploration of biological abnormalities and crime.
Psychiatric research is moving more and more into
neurochemistry and away from other theories. That
wave of research is slowly moving into the study of
murder and criminality.

There is a downside to the new emphasis on biology. As a group, psychiatrists have (I think unfortunately) become less fascinated with personality, history, and emotion, and more intrigued with chemistry and the neuron. There are, thankfully, many exceptions and even a few of us who believe that the biological and psychological approaches are not contradictory.

It is reasonable to question the assumption that criminality is not due to biology. Many criminals have a history of minor or major insults to their brains. At least in children, such injuries may relate to the syndrome of hyperactivity and decreased attention in school. This syndrome has been linked to a variety of behavior problems. A major difficulty in studying this problem in adult or juvenile offenders is that living a criminal life often leads to fights and drugs, two important sources of minor and major brain injury. So it is unclear which came first.

Many psychiatrists stop at this juncture. Psychiatry has a history of finding a good treatment, and then turning the treatment inside out to come up with a theory to explain behavior. Freud found that talking with patients, if structured in a number of ways to promote unrestricted conversation on conflicted areas of the patient's history, could help to alleviate psychosomatic problems. He then reasoned (in part) that the childhood conflicts that he found in the psychoanalysis might be causative, a perfectly reasonable but not necessarily true assumption. If one of his patients had a symptom that had a biological abnormality as a major cause, a psychologically stressful event may have brought the symptom to life. This set of events makes sense, because our brain is most likely to show an emotional difficulty if it is stressed. A patient might try hard at working around a biological difficulty, for example, by understanding the stress that tipped it off, so that similarly vexing stresses are handled better and the symptom may recede. Thus, at least on a theoretical basis, the primarily biological problem could be treated psychologically and vice versa. Yet even this view is simplistic. There is no reason to assume that such things are separate. Psychological events are also biological and vice versa. Stress causes measurable changes in the chemistry of the body. Therefore, the psychological and biological events may merely be outer and inner parts of the same event. Abused children suffer from this convergence. They may be hit enough to develop brain damage, even seizures. And, their life in an unpredictable, violent family causes them to learn that the past is traumatic memories and the future is possibly worse. In addition, they become agents in the commerce of violence. While it is thankfully probable that most victims of childhood violence do not become violent themselves, it seems to be common that violent perpetrators were often victims. Such an observation is difficult to quantify, since abuse victims tend to hide their histories and, on the other hand, convicts lie about their past. While violence is not all caused in the family, it does begin at home at an alarming rate.

The careful and insistent reader may ask, "Well, what do you think causes mental abnormalities? Brain chemistry, the family, or inner emotional struggles?" As is obvious to all but those who choose to make a career in this area, I think that it is all three. I first realized the depth of this complex truth and the intellectual and emotional rigor required to maintain such a belief when I worked with a young man who first complained only of depression. Daren (who is not a murderer) had married at a young age. He steadfastly maintained that he loved his wife, and that all would be well with him if we could "lick" this depression. Freud pointed out the importance of hidden meanings in the choice and even slips of words; I should have noticed that *lick*

was a word that meant "beat," but also implied a positive sense—kissing or fondling with the tongue. We followed his stated objective and we were able to partially lift his depression through medications and psychotherapy. In the therapy, however, it slowly became clear that Daren was ambivalent about losing his depression. It enabled him to distance himself from his older and domineering wife. He had married her just after he dropped out from college. His parents did not know that he had left school. He was confused, unsure whether to tell them, to try again at another school, or to get a job. He met his wife at that point, and she seemed to have all the answers. She helped him to get a job as a mechanic; he eventually worked his way into owning his own repair shop. Over time, Daren realized that his wife had served as something of a substitute parent, and he resented her attempts to make all the decisions, a trait that he admitted he desired at the beginning. Of course, these issues had their basis earlier in life. Daren's father had been a depressed, medically ill man, who slowly gave up on life, allowing (and, in a sense, demanding) that his wife take over. Daren loved his father for his sad, sweet views of the world but resented him for not trying. Similarly, he felt obligated to his mother for raising him, but resented her for not demanding anything of his father.

When I first met Daren, there was little mention of his family or difficulties with his wife. Daren wanted to believe and temporarily convinced me that it was "just depression." Thus, it appeared to be an illness that has strong biological underpinnings, effects, and treatments. I first thought of Daren as a man with a biological problem, until he slowly revealed the family-based and internal conflicts. I often silently thank Daren for helping me to relearn what one of my mentors tried to tell me long ago—that patients bring to the first meeting with a psychiatrist only what they are able to show at the moment. That first glimpse may encompass a piece of the problem from which the rest follows neatly, or it may be something that bears little resemblance to the trouble underneath. This lesson was very important for my later work with murderers, who may do worse than conceal their true feelings and hide their history. They also lie.

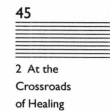

3

Meeting the
Murderer

MURDER IS UNCOMMON. Yet the television news seems to report one or more murders each night. Almost every murder receives some publicity, and murders with more than one victim receive widespread news coverage. Death by illness or accident is overwhelmingly more common but not newsworthy, unless the victim is famous. Similarly, any mental illness present in a murderer is given great attention; in fact, most people with mental illness are not violent. The spotlights of journalism are on murder, making the perceived rate of death by murder seem to be higher than it is.

We fear murder and are fascinated by it. One can easily imagine a person who smokes cigarettes and eats a high-fat diet, yet considers an elaborate alarm and surveillance system a necessity. To compound the enigma, it is also easy to imagine the same individual enjoying murder mysteries and thrillers on the television in his or her home fortress.

The point here is not that efforts at protecting yourself from violence are foolish. Indeed, it is understandable that we wish to strive to prevent death at the hands of other people. In addition, when we view the many causes of death that are outside human control, a glance back at murder would seem to find it to be more easily prevented than other causes. We can't tell viruses, bacteria, or genetics what to do, but shouldn't we be able to control ourselves? Death by intent seems senseless.

Our failure to control ourselves is a source of great worry. This inability to curb violence has led to deep fears about the state of humankind. Among other things, the lust for violence in Western societies has called into question the concept of progress that held that industrialized nations were somehow more highly evolved than other, simpler, "less developed" nations. There is a growing acceptance of the ideas of revisionist historians, who have suggested the characterization of indigenous populations as backwards, primitive, or barbaric is inside out, since more violence was done to these people by European settlers than vice versa. In addition, recent evidence has yielded an increasing appreciation of many of these cultures as far more complex, ecologically minded, and balanced than previously imagined.

These theories have led a fervent return to an age-old question—whether human beings are inherently good or evil. The new incarnation of this debate centers on whether we are originally violent creatures by virtue of evolution, or whether our violence is a product of our move away from our original habitat to the profound stress of civilization and interdependency. Perhaps a simple lifestyle was based on more realistic needs and strivings.

We may not be prepared for the complexity involved or the frustration inherent in depending on a large human and artificial network for sustenance, shelter, and communication. I have seen a few striking examples of the clinical consequences of these issues. I treated a young woman who had no overt symptoms of mental illness when she was allowed to work on her family's isolated farm. She thought unusual thoughts, such as that she communicated with the souls of the farm animals. However, these thoughts did not impair her work or cause her or her family great distress. Indeed, this thinking only came to my attention when her family decided to take an extended trip away from home.

They pressured her to join them. Reluctantly, she did. Away from the pastoral life of home, she became more psychotic, eventually openly displaying symptoms of her delusions. She was admitted to the hospital. Importantly, a previous episode had occurred on an earlier trip away from home and had resolved when she returned to her usual life.

A number of state psychiatric hospitals in the United States used to have large farms where patients worked and spent time. Most, if not all, of the farms have been closed. In some cases, the land was taken away for other purposes. Some farmers became angry about the competition. Most sadly, some advocates of patients' rights thought that all such work was abusive, often leading to the substitution of lassitude and cigarettes in the same hospitals today.

I am not suggesting that we embark on a simplistic retroevolution or that farming is a cure-all for mental illness or murder. We don't know how to prevent murder. Sometimes, our fascination with the topic seems to reach so deep that I wonder if we want it to stop. Murder is a fascinating taboo. It is a topic, like sex, that is both vigorously approached and avoided.

The murderer, however, is not approached. He or she is to be avoided. This choice seems stunningly obvious; we don't associate with murderers because we do not want to be killed. While this explanation is clearly true, there may be more to our avoidance. To look for the other roots of this avoidance, imagine a teenager who idolizes a pop singer. All the teenager wants is to meet and talk with the star. If, by chance, he is able to meet the singer in a social situation and finds her to be boring or superficial, he may not only be disappointed in the star, but also the disappointment might extend to the value of pop music, the judgment of his friends, and the images created by the media. Any parent

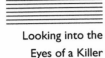

might find his or her heart warmed by these changes. But it may be that there are certain assumptions that we fear challenging within adult society.

Entering work in close contact with murderers requires breaking, or perhaps transcending, certain taboos. While I might like to flatter myself by believing that the reasons for this investigation were scientific curiosity and an avid willingness to examine hypotheses, there are probably less desirable characteristics that entered into my decision to begin this work. It took me a long time to realize that part of my willingness to meet and examine these people related to a long history of episodes of foolish bravery.

The worst of these episodes involved my choice of an apartment in medical school. When I was looking at the apartment in the evening, I thought that it was on the edge of a decent neighborhood. Actually, it was in the center of a troubled neighborhood where a police officer had been murdered. A Hispanic man had been convicted of the crime, but many of the predominantly Hispanic residents did not believe that he was guilty. The neighborhood was angry at the police. The officers, in turn, took an unofficial hands-off attitude toward the area. Drug dealers came in and soon ruled the neighborhood. Cocaine sales occurred on every corner, including mine. One day, I left the hospital an hour or two early because I was developing the flu. It was a steamy day in late spring. I had to take two different buses to get home. Both were crowded. I stood holding the overhead bar as the bus lurched through the streets. As it rocked back and forth, I felt more ill. By the time I walked from the bus stop to my block, I was feverish and fatigued. I turned the corner, ready to go through the door, up the stairs, and climb in bed. But sitting on the steps were two men. Standing over them was a well-dressed man with a revolver drawn and aimed at them. He was asking them questions in an angry tone, but I couldn't hear the queries or answers from the corner. I paused, feeling sick. I didn't know if the man with the gun was a police officer or a criminal. Given the police department's recent behavior, the latter seemed more likely. I briefly reviewed my options. The nearest friend's house was at least another bus ride away, and my fellow medical students might not be home yet from their hospital duties. There was no other door to the building, not even a fire escape. As the sun beat down and my patience faded, a fit of foolish and feverish bravery caught me. I brushed by the men, saying "Excuse me, I live here." As planned, I went upstairs and off to bed.

I have reviewed this story many times. It leads me to worry about my entrance into the field of forensic psychiatry. According to one of the professors who taught me, many psychiatrists enter this area because of a relentless tendency to avoid boredom. Working with criminals is rarely boring, but this lack of patience also leads to daily brushes with danger. In the early days of my work in this area, this danger was something that I superficially acknowledged but, on a deeper level, blithely ignored. My fever as a medical student was paralleled by an enthusiastic exploration of the teachings of my professors and the histories and psyches of my patients. But by looking deeply into the thoughts of these patients that society shuns, my memory brought me back to the steps of the apartment building years before to learn about myself.

I was initially more reluctant to work with these patients. When I was in training, I was required to admit patients to a large state hospital when on-call. As part of my duties, I had to work on the nights and weekends when other people did not want to work. One nighttime responsibility involved driving to the forensic ward, an austere brick building with barred windows and a paved yard with a high fence. The sound of

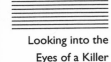
the door buzzer and the clank of the nurse's keys echoed in the long halls. Inside, the hall led to a large, messy staff room with one wall taken up by flickering black-and-white television sets. This room was the last site of frivolity on the journey. The staff were safely separated in this room from the patients by three tall, locked doors. Content to watch on the closed-circuit monitors, they quietly joked about how the night was going and the potential challenges I was to face in examining the night's admission.

A staff member accompanied me out of the room and acted as my guide through the hollow labyrinthine passageways. They were nearly dark and faintly damp, and lined with the large yellow-green tile frequently used in the hallways of old schools. Once past the first locked door, my guide's mood always changed. Now serious and quiet, he or she walked slowly ahead, carefully and mechanically opening each heavy door and shutting it securely behind me. Though there were few intersections, I would wait again to be led, as though a dark pit lay somewhere ahead. In this way, we would proceed to a unit where the new patient was housed. Despite the many nights that I was called for this somber duty, I never remembered the way.

Once at the unit, the patient was summoned. While I waited, eyes peered at me through the small windows of the other rooms or through the smoke coming from a crowded patient lounge. My task was guided by highly structured forms on which I was to write my findings from a physical and mental status examination. Although repetitive copying on an old machine made the sheets blurry and off-center, the forms had been carefully executed to limit the potential for early judgments or editorializing. The unit treated prisoners with mental illness but also served as the site of evaluation for the insanity defense. The older psychiatrists who pronounced such judgments did not want any young

trainees writing something down in the chart that they
would be at pains in court to explain (or contradict). I
saw this tendency to limit information in many guises
as I explored the intersection of law and psychiatry.
Many physicians enter this area reluctantly. Frankly,
some doctors are ill-suited for testimony. Informing a
judge or jury about psychiatry requires the ability to
translate arcane and ambiguous information into readily comprehensible language. The challenge, however,
is to avoid oversimplifying the information. Psychiatry
is a mélange of subtle grays, whereas the law is black
and white. The verdict is guilty or not guilty, and insistent attorneys want yes or no answers. Timid or cor-
rupted souls find it impossible to resist the temptation
of converting the complexities of patients to artful sim-
plicities. After all, psychiatry is about people and their
lives. Judgments in this field are highly dependent on
one's frame of reference. Even the layman's simple
question, "Doc, is he or she crazy?" cannot be answered
without an investigation into the cultural and social
understanding of the unscientific concept of "crazi-
ness." One sign of a system that yearns for simple answers (when there may be none) is an attempt to limit
information. What we choose not to know may indeed
hurt someone.

Nonetheless, despite the terseness of the hospital's
form, my initial reluctance, and the pull of the other responsibilities in the long night in a large state hospital,
I found myself lingering to talk further with these patients. When I arrived at the unit, the chart contained
only a brief, initial nursing evaluation. The patient
might be charged with anything from murder to tres-
passing, and his or her state of mental health ranged
from coy intelligence to agitated psychosis. Often bored
from days or weeks in jail and a long ride to the hospital, most were eager to tell a full story. A call from that
unit always piqued my curiosity. I never knew what

mysteries lay at the end of my journey through those cold corridors.

I am not the only one fascinated with murder. Recently, the nation, or much of it, was transfixed by the coverage of the O. J. Simpson trial and other cases. Details of the lives of the witnesses and even the jurors seemed to be fascinating enough to dominate the supermarket tabloids and their television equivalents. There is perhaps something very compelling about the fall from grace of a sports hero, a seemingly distraught mother, and other people who seemed to be likable and good. Such people are symbols of strong American values. Contemplating the possibility that they have lied and are really "monsters" is chilling and fascinating. One could argue that the focus on the details represents an attempt to understand the fall, to learn to prevent it from happening to us, or to tell the wolf from the sheep. But, I think that the details may also obfuscate the issue; we may get lost in the drama and the characters, and lose sight of the chilling question that drew us in to begin with: If they did such a thing, who can we trust?

Perhaps like the rest of us, I didn't examine these issues in the beginning. My decision to spend more time with certain patients seemed to happen almost accidentally. For more cerebral reasons, I had decided to specialize in the study of the intersections of psychiatry, law, and violence. When I investigated training sites, I was focused more on the mentor than the work. I found a brilliant and supportive teacher, but his program placed me again in a correctional facility for much of each week. I started there, focused more on academic issues such as research ideas and the application of knowledge gained elsewhere to a new population that I did not know. I was green, and the correctional setting was essentially new to me.

It was full of murderers. While the majority of the patients were less violent and probably more mentally ill than criminal, there was a group of very dangerous patients. The sheer number of them led to a denial of the danger, perhaps a numbing. But, when I saw one patient alone, the story and the feeling in the room always broke through the denial that allowed me to come back each day. Part of the fascination occurred because nearly every patient challenged my assumptions and ethics. I expected only to be horrified by these people, but they evoked a full range of emotions.

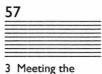

3 Meeting the
Murderer

4

Boredom behind
the Headlines

ARNOLD WAS a slightly built man. He stood straight but weakly, like a frail dancer. Always polite, he was somewhat deferential, although not apologetic. He asked questions about procedure, where to sit, the expected length of the interview, and the nature of its content. These inquiries were never insistent or the least bit rude. Rather, he was trying to find a sense of propriety in prison.

No matter how apparently inconsequential, any question posed to Arnold was met with a furrowed brow and a thoughtful, detailed reply. Indeed, details seemed to fill both his mind and any time spent with him. He began our interview by saying that he had been born in "a town that is no longer a town, really. I guess it was always part of a little bit larger town, but people considered it a separate town. But, later, after I moved away, the towns grew and the borders were less clear. At one time, the post office there had the name of the smaller town, but when they moved the post office, the new one had just the name of the larger town. There still are some stores there with the name of the town, but only the old-timers know what it means. You see, then, I was born in a town that's not a town anymore." When I asked about his parents, he replied along the lines that his mother had "grown up in Chicago. She was part of an old family there. Her father had started some kind of business, shipping it was, I think. I don't know what part of Chicago she was from, because I have never visited it myself, although I think I should someday. It is a large city, I guess, I think that

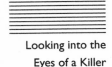
now they say that Los Angeles is the second largest city in the country, but Chicago used to be. So, she grew up there. She was a city girl. From the pictures, she was a pretty woman, and I think that she could have had dates with various men, but her father was very protective. Part of it was that she had some kind of disease when she was a child, and her father and mother thought that she was going to die then. She, my mother, I mean, said that they always thought that she was sickly. They didn't want her doing anything to get sick. I think she said they even wanted her to stay indoors when it was cold, which must be pretty hard in Chicago, which is pretty cold, I understand. So, I think that she was a bit sheltered. . . ." Similarly, a description of an acquaintance would include a physical description; an inventory of his ancestry, occupation, assets, and family; and his habits of speech and behavior. Inevitably, such a description would remind Arnold of some other story, also replete with great detail as to its location, timing, and characters. These divergences could build on each other, stories within descriptions within descriptions within stories. Eventually, if allowed, Arnold would pick up the thread again and relate the story back to the issue at hand. But the significance or illuminative value of the story never merited the details. They were details for details' sake. If he realized that he had made any mistake in the details, Arnold would correct himself, unaware that anyone other than he had forgotten the context of the subplot that contained the error. In a word, Arnold was boring.

He had grown up on a small farm and had found solace in a lonely, barren childhood by driving his father's tractor. Repeating this exercise indefinitely, he became a long-distance truck driver, a life that took him to many towns, leading to many details. At home, he paid his bills and was a supportive, albeit physically and emotionally distant, husband. Secretly, his wife resented Arnold's affection for his younger sister, a vivacious young woman who seemed to bring out his more jovial, sporting side. Unknown to his wife, Arnold had sexually molested his sister on numerous occasions when she was a teenager. Although this behavior had stopped, Arnold had replaced it with the rape of similar younger and often vivacious women. The rapes always occurred in cities a far distance from his home, and Arnold meticulously disguised himself and escaped from the scenes. Perhaps he would have been caught sooner had all of his attacks occurred in one state, but the distance and lack of evidence helped him to elude discovery. On at least two occasions, the victim pulled off the ski mask that Arnold wore to cover his face. On both occasions, he killed them, hiding the bodies in isolated places far from the scene of the crime.

Although he would not discuss this issue, over time, Arnold seemed to have lost some of the excitement in this other, brutal side of his life. Perhaps the repeated attacks no longer satisfied his urges. He became more violent and began to rape closer to home.

All the while, his employers and family suspected nothing. He was respected and appreciated by his boss and fellow truck drivers, partially because he would volunteer to take the longest distance drive. But he also garnered respect for being quiet, easygoing, and respectful. He even gave a donation to an organization working for the prevention of child abuse. For him, the two parts of his life were completely walled off from one another. In his regular life, he was never rude or impertinent, never violent or aggressive. All of those impulses were kept for the other life. But the rapes became like gambling; he needed more and more risk to become excited. All the while, he was otherwise predictable, well-liked and, of course, boring.

Finally, Arnold was caught. A young woman escaped after seeing part of his face, distinguishing marks

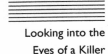
on his body, and his car. The arrest shocked his friends. As the drivers who had accepted him struggled with the news and the resultant attention, many suspected that Arnold had some unidentified medical illness that would explain his Jekyll-and-Hyde life and exonerate him.

I came to meet Arnold in a manner opposite to that of his supporters. When we met, he already had been convicted. I expected him to be strikingly evil-looking and, in some way, obviously lewd. Instead, I found a small man who outwardly seemed to be deadly only in terms of boredom. Over time, this presentation began to make an odd sense. Arnold seemed to fill up his normal life with details, both to forget and to delay the rapes. I believe that he tried to keep out that dangerous part from awareness, but it would come back. A perhaps frightening but certainly gnawing and titillating urge would grow until he raped again, after which he seemed to dive further into details and a hardly equivalent penance of minor good deeds and meticulous service to his employers.

The sense that I made of Arnold was that he kept his aggressive and sexual urges out of his normal life with his obsessive attention to details. Meanwhile, in the dark recesses of his mind, the drives grew, slowly and persistently. At some level, Arnold understood his impulses and attacks to be bad. He avoided them, and they grew. Their only expression was horrible, a grossly perverted sense of his attraction to his sister and perhaps a deflected punishment of what he viewed as her tempting him. His arrest, trial, and conviction received strong media attention. His picture was broadcast nearly nightly on the evening news for several weeks, and the gruesome story was told and retold. Initial errors of detail were eventually corrected—I wondered if Arnold called the broadcast stations himself. However, the media never captured his character very well. They implied that his fellow drivers' trust in him was due to ignorance, and they portrayed him as a seething monster. His criminal actions were indeed monstrous. However, the public never suspected the true horror. His evil lust existed in a dark corner within an otherwise reliable and uninteresting little man. The persona was not a front, not a falsehood, but a shield. What was horrible about this revelation for me was the degree to which the two sides could be walled off from one another. We are all sexual creatures, and I think it true that we unconsciously think something sexual frequently. Yet for months after meeting Arnold, I was sensitive to even the most subtle lecherous glance of an older man for a young woman or girl. The slightest hint of a smile brought on a mild but persistent wave of nausea. It is not that I intellectually thought it wrong for an older man to find a young woman attractive. It is just that the meeker the man was, the more he reminded me of Arnold. If his eyes averted quickly when the woman glanced to see who was looking, I could see Arnold's small, weak, but evil eyes. Though the glance of the man might be innocent, I could only imagine rape in his mind. Arnold had made a mockery of meekness.

When I was growing up, my stepfather regaled me with his summaries of the classic radio shows. He told of the famous comedies and dramas, how families would gather around the radio to listen. Television was a disappointment to him; it took away his own images of how the characters looked, how the hero sauntered into the room, the look on the villain's face when he was caught red-handed. One of his favorite shows was *The Shadow,* in which a mysterious representative of the world's conscience solved crime by knowing the criminals better than they knew themselves. The show opened with haunting music and a resounding voice echoing, "Who knows what evil lurks in the heart of men? . . . The Shadow knows. . . ." As a psychiatrist, and especially as a forensic psychiatrist, it can seem

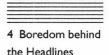

easy to know that evil, to trace the origins and sources of problematic behavior. Hearing stories of crime over and over leads to a sense, if not a better formed theory, of the sources of criminality in any given person. Over time, I developed an ability to anticipate the direction of a criminal's conversation. I became able to predict some aspects of his or her early life based on what I knew from the written record about his or her behavior as an adult. As this ability became sharpened, evaluations became easier. I felt grounded and less confused than I had felt earlier in my journey.

Arnold humbled me greatly. Although I knew that there were many ways in which appearances could deceive, Arnold offered as close an example of a Jekyll-and-Hyde split as I ever hope to see. The normal half of his life was not a ruse, in my opinion. He simply was very successful at keeping his prodigious supply of evil out of it (at least visibly). Since dealing with him, I am much more attuned to the subtleties of personality, the nonverbal cues and pauses in conversation, the hints of aggression and exasperation in the humble and polite among us.

Jungian theorists have been interested in the shadow aspects of people for a long time. Some believe that all of us have walled-off parts of ourselves caged up in our minds because they are unacceptable. In a difficult part of my life, I felt that events led me to confront and meet with one part of my own shadow self. Unlike Arnold, I was not acting out the shadow's wishes. But at a time when I felt devalued and angry, my shadow's cries for vengeance were heard, at first distantly, then more clearly. I had the sense that this part of me had been screaming for a long time. When my level of distress broke through the psychological wall I had around "him," he seemed like a loathsome character, wanting to kick, punch, and insult those who falsely appeared to support me, but did not. Yet in his insults, which were contradictory to my usual nature and behavior, there was a grain of truth. Maybe more than a grain. As I attempted to "listen" to this part of myself, my eyes opened to the ways in which seemingly nice people had failed to support me. It almost seemed that listening caused the "voice" of this part of myself to quiet, for the aggression and then the bluster to moderate. Suddenly, I saw things more clearly, and saw how the polite behavior of ingenuine administrators contained more venom than a seemingly fearsome and previously hidden part of myself.

Paralleling my search to understand Arnold, people who knew him searched for a reason for his behavior, including theories best kept in the supermarket tabloids. One citizen wrote a letter stridently suggesting an explanation based on the sighting of a pack or two of wild dogs in the town. They had allegedly killed a rabbit, and the letter writer was convinced they may also have bitten Arnold, and that he and they were rabid.

On a less speculative but more disturbing level, there were those who wondered about his victims. One local matron had spied one of the young women at a steamy movie with a date, and had decided that any young lady with the moral turpitude to see such a film had asked for rape. I strongly disagree with society's desire to explore the possibility that a rape victim tempted the rapist. No set of seductive clothing warrants rape. Yet the persistence of this theme makes me wonder if it is a theme for rapists. In other words, I think that rapists like Arnold find it easier to find explanations for their wrongful behavior in the outside world than they do by looking inside. Arnold admitted to this type of thinking in court, noting that he thought that a young woman's eye contact or brief exchange of conversation indicated sexual desire. Perhaps even before the act, the rapist is convinced that the blame lies in the victim. Perhaps part of the reason for the unforgivable and yet-to-be-eradicated tendency for courts to explore these issues is this woeful misapplication of blame by the criminal.

But do men and women subtly attract each other? While I do not wish to strongly support the notion that all men are rapists, I do suspect that we all have at least nanograms of the stuff that perversions are made of. I suspect that Arnold believed that his victims tempted him. In a sublime way, he may be right. Normal people allow touches of aggression and sexuality into their life. Much of our motivation, if you even half-believe Freud, may come from such wellsprings and then get converted into friendship, ambitions, and what many term "innocent" flirting. Disallowing this normal expression might lead to a welling up of these feelings. The thoroughly normal degree of this "microflirtation" might seem alien and a completely inappropriate invitation to murder for a man like Arnold. As such, it is often the rapist's contention that such subliminal attention should exculpate him. I wish that the courts did not enter into lengthy, difficult debates to determine the degree of this temptation, which is often at a level that may lead the rest of us to be friendly or smile. It hardly can be an excuse for rape. What is frightening is that society also can take this all-or-nothing attitude about sex and aggression that so centrally characterized Arnold. His case seems to point out how a tendency toward overcleansing of such "bad" impulses can lead to the opposite of the desired result. A more comical result of similar efforts occurred when the television programmers attempted to reduce violence on television by not having characters die on screen. The result was that children saw high-speed car accidents result in uninjured characters. It was not an avoidance of violence, but an avoidance of its results. Television also has not learned subtlety.

5

The Thriller Killer

CHARLIE SAT QUIETLY waiting for me. When I called him into the interview room, a thin, almost silly smile took over his face. The story he told seemed plausible at first. He considered himself a security expert, and he was hired to help an armored car company reduce theft. As part of the job, he rode in the armored cars and came to know some of the thieves that preyed on them. He also came to know many of the members of the local police. In his description of his activities, his casual air turned serious as he began to talk about the robberies.

The series of robberies had a certain pattern to them, he explained. "They were precise, well-planned. I was real careful. I investigated these things, these people who were heisting the trucks. Now, to do that, I mean, how would you do it? You would have to talk to the thieves, if you could, just like you are talking to me, just like the cops try to talk to the thieves to get them to say something they shouldn't or put a little pressure on them so they screw up. That's how it works." When a group of thieves was eventually arrested, he was implicated, too. He was arrested and convicted. "Now, I really can't tell you too much about the investigation, because it is still in process in many ways. You know, they're still looking for some of the guys involved and I don't want to screw that up. I spent a lot of time on this investigation."

Wait a moment, I thought, didn't he say that he worked for the armored car company? Of course, he answered, when the question was voiced, but he also worked closely with the police. An ingenuine smile fed my doubt. He said that the insurance company that had sent him to the armored car company was sorry to see him go; he was such a valued employee. Slowly, an image began to congeal in my mind as Charlie continued his story. I pictured him as a small-time thief who had big aspirations. He tried to escape prosecution and blame by characterizing himself as an investigator who had been framed. It was a plot worthy of television and perhaps derived from it.

My theory began to lose ground when sexual themes emerged. He began to blame a young woman. He began describing her: "She was tall, with blonde hair. It was long, you know, like in the magazines. The hair was dyed, but what the hell, she looked great. Who cares? Her eyes, you wouldn't believe them, better than the women in magazines or TV, I mean it. She had this look like she wanted to do it right there and then, and at the same time, like it really didn't matter. She looked sort of innocent, but she wasn't. Those eyes made you want her; they reeled you in like a fishing line, but you couldn't really read them. They were like one-way mirrors, because she had the whole thing figured, I think. Maybe she was lying all along. You see, I'm still trying to figure it out. From a few feet, she looked like a little girl, or maybe in high school or college. Only real close could you see she was older. She wasn't real wrinkled; you could tell that she had been around, somehow that she knew what she was doing. You could see that she was in charge, she was powerful. I guess that side came clearer as I got to know her. She was kind of teasing me, and I liked it for a while, but then I could see that she was no good. I still wanted to get to know her better, but I knew she wasn't trying to help me, that she was playing with me or something. So, I thought, two can play at that game, so I started playing, too. I think that she didn't really know who she was messing with. But, you see, being tough with her, that's what she needed, she kept coming around. She got what she needed." He implied that this woman had died, but he wouldn't answer any more questions about her.

He did admit that one of the thieves' girlfriends was brutally murdered. Then, changing course, he boldly stated that he had helped the police solve a series of murders of young women because he knew criminals, he knew "how they think." He said that he could reconstruct the murder, and in this way, find the necessary evidence. He again smiled and said, "It's almost like I'm clairvoyant." The thought came to me and I dismissed it. It came again, then it sizzled. I was fascinated and horrified. It began to make sense that he could only be so helpful if he was the murderer.

He denied this assertion, but the smile appeared again. I began to notice that the smile and stare grew in intensity when my head turned or if I glanced downward to my notes. His sensitivity to my questions and guesses grew more obvious. If I called any question to a point, he backed off, smiling. It was as if he knew that I knew.

I began to believe that Charlie was a serial murderer. He was quite knowledgeable about the police and not illiterate in matters related to psychiatry. He was exquisitely sensitive and attuned to my demeanor and opinion; he met any equivocality on my part with inquisition. In this way, he tried to find my interests and fulfill them, as well as my worries, which he tried to tantalize. Over the course of the interview, he did pique my interest in a disturbing manner. He referred to his victims as though they were the subject of his investigation rather than violence. It is as if he were the author of a thriller novel about serial murder, and he was providing the script. Given my interest in writing, I worried that he gleaned this feature from me. It seemed like a dream—an oddly familiar mix of my interests with my fears. If Arnold had cut the shadow side of himself off from the rest of his life in order to live it in secret, then with Charlie, it felt as if I was meeting some darker, unimagined aspect of mine. But, just as quickly as these thoughts came, Charlie's discourse veered off, beyond my personal nightmare, bringing to life a larger one.

He was fascinated by the media. Charlie's interest raised a great concern for me. His story became more and more like a television plot as he told it. Indeed, I was part of it, a reluctant detective.

While psychiatrists and psychologists sometimes work with investigative teams, those evaluating someone for the insanity defense are intended to be far removed from police concerns. The job is not to "solve" the crime by finding out who did it, or to gather evidence to seal a conviction. The intended role is to understand the mental motivation. Not "who done it," but why. The doctor's job is not to help the court decide whether the defendant did the crime, but whether an illness led him or her to it. Nonetheless, figuring out that motivation involves gathering a lot of details about the crime. Psychiatrists are trained listeners, experts in rapport. Sometimes defendants tell us things that they didn't tell the police or even their lawyer. From a legal perspective, they shouldn't. Looking for the presence of insanity is supposed to be separate from criminal investigation, clean of it. It is something like the way that the jury is supposed to not know of the crime before they appear in court. Sometimes, neither of these attempts to keep things clean works.

So, the law has erected some other safeguards, some walls of protection. In some jurisdictions, insanity evaluations don't occur until after the defendant has decided to plead insanity. That means he or she essentially has admitted to the crime, but the evaluation may occur years after the crime, after the attorney has filed

motions, considered other pleas, and decided to pursue
an insanity verdict. Places that ask the question earlier
have the doctor see the defendant within a few months,
sometimes even within days of the crime, when the information is fresh. Some of the states that allow these
earlier evaluations seal the report until the plea is entered—the information is gathered early but not available to the system until later. Still others allow the
reports to be read but bar the entrance of information
from the report as damning evidence. In a system in
which plea bargains are increasingly the means of dealing with criminal cases, I worry that information from
the report might seep in and poison the proceedings,
even though it is technically barred. Let's say that a defendant is arrested for a serious crime. He says little to
the police when he is arrested, and less after his attorney is present. The evidence is equivocal—not a clear
conviction or acquittal. Since there is a mental illness,
his attorney allows him to talk with an examining psychiatrist. In the course of that evaluation, he admits to
incriminating information. Because this information
also relates to the question of the role mental illness
might have played in his behavior, the psychiatrist puts
it in the report. The defendant's attorney can be sure
that it is not used to convict him, but if both sides see it,
wouldn't it change the plea bargain?

All of this controversy places the psychiatrist in a
precarious position—sometimes knowing important,
maybe convicting information. I have tended to make
my reports long on details of the illness and short on the
crime. But it is harder to know where the line is when I
talk on the phone with an inquisitive prosecutor. I may
know what is in the police report, but keeping the discussion within the bounds of the prosecutor's knowledge is tricky and feels a little deceitful.

This situation is one of those confusing conflicts
of psychiatry and the law. The statutes in some areas

have created some low, leaky walls to hold information. I often have felt unsure, as if I am floating above those walls, and I don't know what to say. In between the extremes of telling all and saying nothing is always a purportedly reasonable compromise, but the depths of this issue are murky. I was beginning to perceive deeper layers of uncertainty. My professional journey had opened up burning questions.

With Charlie, things were worse than usual. The charge that brought him to the evaluation was not murder, but related to the armored car thefts. I suspected him of guilt in unsolved crimes. He never gave me anything solid, but the story was compelling and convincing.

Sometimes, patients in psychotherapy will tell of a past crime that they committed without discovery. Generally, with exceptions such as child abuse, the therapist is not compelled to disclose the information. That secrecy may be disturbing, but there are strong, historical roots protecting the sanctity of the information shared in psychotherapy. Sometimes, the crime occurred long ago. Other times, the story may be a lie or a delusion, or if it is true, the patient decides to confess to authorities. The situation is perhaps always uncomfortable to the therapist.

But I wasn't Charlie's therapist. I struggled with what to do. One supervisor seemed to think that because I wanted to meet a serial killer, I had superimposed one onto the vague ramblings of an artful thief. I looked at that possibility—was I writing the television show? It was true that the evidence was more suggestive than conclusive, but I remained unsure. Part of me wanted to pursue the story and become an unofficial investigator. I could scour the newspapers on microfilm and try to piece the few details together.

I was lost. The gap between psychiatry and the law had widened into an abyss. I pondered, I worried. I

discussed the issue with colleagues and supervisors.
We eventually decided that I did not have enough information to make a definite conclusion, and that I
could not tell anyone anyway.

That decision was reasonable, but Charlie still
haunts me. It is partially because of that lingering
question, and also because he seemed to be so much
like television. I began to wonder, and then to worry
that he was its product.

To what extent does television contribute to violence? This question has received attention in the form
of research and debate. Researchers have focused primarily on its effects on normal, and more importantly,
troubled children. Some suggest that these children
and some adults with similar difficulties may find a
greater sense of consistency and normality on television than they do in their own chaotic lives. Often
socially isolated, these individuals may find that television may serve as a window into social norms and
values. In short, television may seem normal to them.

But television is not normal. It functions as a passive release for many people, but I worry more about
those who have little in the way of family or other social contact with which to balance and contradict the
media's message. Imagine if a visitor from a less industrialized nation learned the languages of the West but
had no social contact and only learned abut the culture
in the United States and Europe through television.
Among other problems, the news discusses and por-
trays violence with such passivity that it would be hard
to explain why (or if) the culture that produces these
shows doesn't find violence to be normal. Each night,
well-dressed, smiling, and attractive newspeople fit in
a few words on the most recent murders somewhere after the political news and before sports. Characteristi-
cally, the broadcasters display more emotion if the
home team loses in a major sport. The commentators

are numb; they do not react. Similarly, they do not disturb the rhythm of the program to discuss the latest violence. If one turned the sound off, the only cues to the subject matter of the story would be the accompanying graphics and, at times, a modest furrowing of the brow as an unconvincing show of concern. Of course, the drama shows are worse. Violence is frequently portrayed as a form of redress and a means of excitement.

Imagine a horrific worsening of the scenario in which the emissary from another nation uses TV as his or her only source of information. Imagine a child who is fed and bathed, but whose major social interactions and only source of morality come from television. Although the example is exaggerated, children in households with absent, severely depressed, or impaired caretakers may have television as at least the major source of morality. While I cannot imagine and do not propose a complete proscription of violence in the media, the morality of the messages portrayed must be considered. I do not mean that only certain religious or political views should be aired. In my view, the answer is more simple. Television should more reliably portray the realistic outcome of mortal violence—death for the victim, havoc for the family of the victim and perpetrator, and a sad, hard life in prison for the perpetrator.

Charlie did not see that as his future. I think that he had difficulty separating himself from the characters on television. I believe that he wanted to impress an imaginary audience with the clever plot of his story, its perverse sexuality, and swift, unyielding violence. Although I hold Charlie responsible for his actions, I believe that he emulated the morality of television in which sex is often (if gently) violent, and in which closure on all issues occurs in ninety minutes or less. Furthermore, television audiences are taught that fame is success. Without education, and having no athletic skills, Charlie may have found his most available (and possibly only) means to notoriety. Charlie's trouble may lie more in the lack of a human network as a child and as an adult than in the effects of the media. Nonetheless, the thematic equivalence between Charlie and much of the nightly offerings on television haunt me and keep me wondering if he would be fascinated with violence and possibly a killer if television were not around.

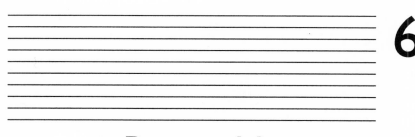

6

Beyond Insanity

MARK HAD DATED several women before but he saw something in Kathy that he had never seen before. It was as if the good parts of his mother were taken out and placed in a young, vibrant woman who loved to dance and smile. For reasons beyond him, Kathy also seemed to love Mark. With previous girlfriends, sex had felt dirty. He frequently had smoked marijuana to "get into the mood." The sex seemed "spacey" and fun, but bad at the same time. He didn't use marijuana with Kathy, and sex with her felt better. For Mark, it seemed to be almost holy.

The only negative feelings occurred when Kathy was away, and those moments felt like an ever-constricting hell, each second worse than the last. Any attention that Kathy received from other men felt awful, because his life would, in his mind, simply end if she left. Yet, since her love for him seemed inexplicable and random, might she wake up and decide to go? This worry haunted him and rarely brought about a sense of anger toward Kathy, who he believed had the power to bring a capricious and swift end to the meaning of his life. This worry did not provoke any desire for distance from her; rather, Mark worried to a nearly intolerable degree when they were apart. During the day, his job as a construction worker kept him busy enough to not worry too much about the contact Kathy might have with other men in her work as a receptionist. But the rare night that Kathy took to spend with her girlfriends was too much for him. At least one of Kathy's friends was looking for a boyfriend. Wouldn't she ask

Kathy what she thought of any man that they saw? Wouldn't it be inevitable that Kathy would compare the man with Mark? Couldn't Kathy decide that another man was better, and wouldn't any man die to be with Kathy? Mark tried to keep his worries quiet; he didn't want to seem too worried to Kathy. But he also drank when she went out with her friends, and he couldn't help seeming hurt when she came home. One time, he drank too much and asked her if she had seen any attractive men while she was out. Kathy teased him and said that she had. Not realizing the extent of his worry, Kathy teased him some more, and Mark punched her. She cried and threatened to leave. He apologized profusely and regaled her with phone calls at work, presents, and flowers. He was very mad at himself, because he had thought about asking her not to go out with her friends anymore, and now felt unable to do so.

Mark grew up with a distant, angry father who drank and rarely, but unpredictably, beat his wife and children. His mother doted on Mark and his sisters but felt like a failure because she didn't know how to help her husband. Mark, who physically resembled his father, was a constant reminder of her sense of helplessness. She felt more comfortable with his sisters, although she assuaged her guilt by occasionally spending a weekend doing everything that Mark could imagine wanting to do: a carnival, sports game, and shopping. As he became a teenager, these weekends became more inappropriate, with visits to nightclubs and at least one sexually charged kiss on the lips.

Although Mark might not agree, it appeared that marrying Kathy would fulfill the yearning that he had for his mother while softening the disappointments of that early relationship. He was thrilled when Kathy announced that she was pregnant with their child. They decided to marry after the baby was born because her sister was getting married that year, and Kathy didn't want to diminish the focus on her somewhat shy sister. But the pregnancy seemed to bring problems. Mark became increasingly jealous and couldn't seem to resist provoking minor fights. Kathy then wanted to spend more time recovering with her girlfriends, a process that increased Mark's jealousy. Eventually, he slapped her and she finally moved out. A few months after the baby was born, Kathy began to date another man.

Mark became despondent. He felt that only a reunion with Kathy could help him. He began drinking more and nearly lost his job because he couldn't sleep well. He stalked her. He spent many hours parked outside her house, watching for a glimpse of Kathy, the baby, or her new boyfriend in the window. Much of the time was spent waiting, and it was boring. But his proprietary wishes were partially fulfilled as he watched over his beloved, even if she was with another man. Gradually, he knew all of her movements, the hours that she left for work and came home, even the usual hours when the bathroom light was illuminated. He tried to follow her when she drove in her car, and when she rode with her new boyfriend.

Gradually, his worries became more paranoid. He began to worry that the police were after him. At first, this fear related to a restraining order that Kathy obtained because of his frequent presence and occasional phone call pleading for, or insistently demanding, a reunion. Later, he became convinced that the police were pursuing him for a minor burglary he had committed with friends when he was sixteen. To Mark, the police seemed to watch him constantly but never move in for the arrest. He began to think that they must be planning to find an excuse to kill him, a fear heightened by the fact that Kathy's father was a retired police sergeant. He also began to worry that Kathy and their child were being mistreated by the new boyfriend, a man that reminded Mark of his own father. He began to fantasize about killing the man and rescuing Kathy and their son. When he revealed this thought to Kathy, she called the police. Officers visited Mark and sternly warned him about threats. One of the officers placed his hand on the handle of his service revolver as they left. Mark interpreted this gesture as meaning that he was to be killed soon. He also began to believe that Kathy was brainwashed. As his depression and psychosis deepened, he became convinced that he had to kill Kathy, their child, and himself.

In one sense, the desire to murder represented a desire to rescue Kathy, their son, and himself from a world that he saw as increasingly horrible and wrong. It was also a punishment for the failure of their family to form in the way that he had dreamed. On a less obvious level, it would be a sacrifice giving up the woman he loved as a payment to the overwhelmingly harsh and brutal forces Mark felt all around him. Most hauntingly, the murder, to Mark, was an act of love for a man who felt that sex, like violence, was wrong. To kill her was to kiss her good-bye, a taboo act like his mother's kiss. It was also a demonstration of his sexually charged power, a way of showing that the final act in her life would be from him. Implicit in his thoughts and feelings is a model of gender relations in which women are not people like men, but beings (or objects) to be either revered or reviled. This aspect of Mark's thinking is not psychotic; it is, unfortunately, a commonly held value. Whether placed on pedestals or chained to the cliff to be sacrificed to the beast, women are to be acted upon. Kathy represented so many powerful symbols to Mark that it is difficult to discern whether he ever really knew her, even before he became psychotic. His stalking was tending, as a shepherd does to his flock. Probably due to his own sense of inadequacy, he wanted to own and control Kathy, not know her as she was.

Drunk, tired, and with a sense of inevitability, Mark killed Kathy by stabbing her many times. The baby, luckily, was with Kathy's parents. Mark did not commit suicide because he was convinced that the police would shoot him on sight. Instead, he was arrested as he walked slowly away from Kathy's house.

In prison, Mark continued to be obsessed with Kathy and their child. Although he eventually recovered from a deep depression and the paranoid psychosis, he remained brokenhearted. Although his story is compelling, it was difficult to sit with Mark. He was incessantly vigilant and demanded absolute clarity about any interaction. His remorse was ambivalent and the roots of his anger and violence reached deeper, beyond his insanity. He also had unresolved difficulties with his parents and the disrespect for Kathy that underlay and coexisted with his love. Most personally chilling for me was the degree to which Mark equated murder with love, the way in which he felt that he could select death for Kathy without asking her. Part of the difficulty inherent in Mark's case is the tendency for society to assume that patients with mental illness always (rather than usually) have a good heart underlying their loss of reality. In court, this sense sometimes comes to life as a psychotic patient is portrayed as an innocent child beleaguered by psychosis. Mark's case points out that psychosis may enhance and enact the drama already present, and the drama is not necessarily an innocent one.

7

The Sexuality
of Violence

Ned's childhood was nearly unimaginable. His mother died when he was three. She used heroin and cocaine on a daily basis. At times, the cocaine made her so irritable and high that she used large doses of sedatives to "come down." Needless to say, this dangerous mixing and balancing of drugs was far from scientific. A few times a month, she would use too many sedatives and sleep for days. During these periods, Ned received no care. He was left crying in his crib. Finally, his mother left him with her parents a year before she died of heart disease caused by drugs. His father was unknown. His grandparents were caring but stern and punitive. They also were advanced in years. When he was eight, they died, leaving him with an aunt and uncle. These relatives placed him in a residential program when he began cursing, lying, stealing, and drinking, not long before his tenth birthday. As he passed from program to hospital to program, he progressed to more serious theft, gang involvement, and heavy drug use. At sixteen, Ned was placed in a foster home with the Arnolls. They were a young, religious family who had worked with people like Ned and his mother in substance-abuse treatment. They were firm and made specific demands on Ned. He attended school and the family received a daily report on his behavior. For the first time outside of an institution, Ned had a curfew and chores. His dating hours were restricted. His monetary allowance was tied to his behavior, including improvement in his language. More important, he was frequently checked for drugs, including screens of his urine.

In exchange for adherence to this controlled regimen, Ned received a tremendous amount of support. Eventually, this support became admiration, then love. The Arnolls understood and could tolerate Ned's despair and anger at the same time that they structured his behavior. Besides stopping his use of drugs, the program at the Arnolls led to a absence of stealing and a remarkable reduction in other antisocial behavior. Unfortunately, Mr. Arnoll lost his job. The resultant financial tailspin forced the Arnolls to have to focus the family resources on their natural and adopted children, although they had previously hoped to adopt Ned. He was sent to another foster home, where his old behavior soon returned. Arrests for minor robberies, assaults, and drug charges again began to appear on his record.

Ned didn't date anyone more than once until he was nearly thirty. He had brief sexual encounters with prostitutes or women he met while doing drugs (and rarely saw again). Sex for him was brief and unsatisfying. It was an urge that had to be discharged. But his sexuality also was based on more than physical needs. He had an image, an idea of what it meant to be masculine. It was more than a superficial machismo. To him, a man was hard, unfeeling, and inscrutable: a quiet loner who had no second thoughts and no mercy. Like many of the others in this book, Ned had been sexually violated as an adolescent. At one of the group homes, a repairman that lived nearby was a frequent visitor to the house to make the inevitable repairs in an old house inhabited by young, wild boys. He used his frequent visits to sexually abuse the boys and threaten them into silence. Ned was abused on a number of occasions. Sex had been forced and wrong, and forever remained that way in his mind. Part of the problem was that women, typified by his absent mother, seemed unpredictable and unreliable. Anger and arousal were so intermingled that they would be better named by one term than two. Similarly, sex was violence and vice versa. As an adult, Ned was a loner, always trying to be that unfeeling man. But he experienced sadness and great bouts of rage that he didn't understand. He numbed himself with drugs. Although there were drinking buddies and sexual partners, he lived alone, profoundly alone.

While under the influence of alcohol and probably other drugs, Ned broke into the house of a middle-aged couple. Only the woman was home. He acted on the unspeakable side of fantasy. In an enactment of his love—anger toward his mother, he brutally raped and murdered the woman. For him, they were the same act.

When asked to explain the murder, Ned first tried to tell me that it was "the drugs, all drugs." As he carefully pronounced each word of a practiced history of his drug use, his eyes wandered, studying mine, to see if I was buying his explanation. I was not, and he knew it, even before I told him. After a few more attempts at diversion, he admitted that his initial conscious goal upon entering the house was money. He couldn't find any, and couldn't locate any readily resellable objects, either. The house was in a good neighborhood, and the furniture was of good quality, so it angered him that there was no visible money or items that he could fence. He said to me, "She had a black-and-white TV. Can you believe that this rich old lady had a f---ing black-and-white TV?" It still amazed him that a wealthy person would have an inexpensive television. He took it as a deliberate insult toward him, a planned source of frustration. He did not, and maybe could not, see the connection between the woman and his mother. He tried, as always, to be distant and cool. But his eyes and mouth betrayed him. There was almost a pout—a frustrated and angry boy bent on revenge.

Many groups correctly point out that rape is a violent crime. They perhaps strain the point by sometimes claiming that it is not sexual. This statement is certainly true for the victim but may not be for the perpetrator, although the sexuality of the crime is clearly perverse. Working with murderers (and rapist–murderers), I have become convinced that the opposite conclusion may be more true. Murder, arguably the most extreme form of violence, is often sexual. Of course, the sexuality is not normal; this argument is not meant as an excuse for this behavior. Some people have had such a distorted life and have such a perverse fantasy life that violence is a form of approach. At least, for them, it is perhaps the closest that they can come to another. This statement is so disheartening as to be nauseating. Yet this idea has been reinforced in my mind many times. Some murderers, by virtue of either upbringing or constitution, find that they cannot approach without destroying and, indeed, victims of violence feel that the sanctity of their world has been invaded and destroyed. There is an old phrase that seems tired and pat but captures the essence of this inscrutable pairing of emotions that we otherwise deem to be opposites. For these murderers, the search for companionship is, indeed, the "kiss of death," and tragically, murder is love and hate at once.

Even the paranoid patient who seems to want only to repel everyone may have a hint of sadism—for some deeply paranoid individuals, violence is the only close contact that they have. Classically, the paranoid male was thought by some to fear a homosexual advance and thus reacted to other males with great contrition and avoidance. Nonetheless, some psychoanalytic thinkers believe that, at his core, the paranoid patient may so desire any closeness that he would succumb even to sodomy. Thus, the paranoia is a splint against a near-total loss of control. These thoughts are not easily transferable to homosexuals or women, and they are complex and counterintuitive. Yet there seems to be at least a grain of truth within them. It may be that there is a somewhat more general truth, that paranoid patients want the social contact that they seem to so terribly fear. I better understood this concept when I met Horace. He was thirty when he was hospitalized at a general hospital for appendicitis. As he recovered from a resultant infection, the nurses noticed that he interpreted even the most benign stimulus as evidence of a conspiracy against him. At first, it was thought that he was confused due to his infirm condition and the medications given to him. When he made a brisk physical recovery but began throwing objects at the nursing staff, he was transferred from a general hospital to a psychiatric unit. He subsequently was discharged after a week because he was calm and refused to discuss his condition with anyone.

Back at home, he eked out an existence by working in the back of a warehouse. Each morning, he would arrive at work and pick up a list of the day's shipments in his mailbox. From this list, he would begin loading boxes from shelves onto forklift vehicles. As the forklift drivers were intimidated by his large size and intense stare, they rarely spoke to him. Occasionally, a manager would call back an additional order on the telephone. These were the only direct communications to Horace. Since he ate lunch alone, he was able to be a respected employee who had essentially no human contact at work. This lack of stimuli did not prevent him from fantasy. He was quite convinced that some of the forklift drivers planned to hurt him. He was equally convinced that some of the women who worked at the factory were in love with him, although it was likely that over half of the women in his group of imagined admirers had never seen him. None had spoken with him. At home, Horace kept an audiotaped record of his

perceptions. His tapes about the women were recorded as if he were speaking with them, although he never phoned or approached them. A typical one would sound something like "Lila, I've been seeing you around work. You are the most beautiful woman at the plant. You look especially sweet and sexy in the blue shirt and jeans you wore on Thursday. I know that you have noticed me, too. It's that little twinkle in your eye and the way that you look at me. I know you want me. I want you too. I know what you look like under those blue jeans. I want you to rip off my clothes and I'll rip off yours. I'll hold you hard, not too hard, baby, and you'll look at me and I'll know you want me. Even if you scream, I know it will be screams of pleasure because I know you want me. . . ."

Horace also believed that he could read the intentions of men and generally thought that they meant him harm. One day, Horace was walking on a city street. He had been raised in the country and rarely entered the city. However, he misinterpreted a letter from his insurance company and thought that an announcement of a yearly renewal meant that his policy had been canceled. A series of letters and phone calls failed to reassure him, so Horace drove to the city to speak to the company. He was tense, angry, and uneasy. The city was full of angry faces and threatening noises. Each of these was interpreted by Horace as an attack levied against him. He searched each face as if sizing up the enemy. Each noise startled him and caused him to turn around and face his presumed attacker. As he neared the company's office, which had been difficult for him to find, he was in a state of terror. As he crossed a street, he bumped into a small, old man. Hunched over, the man hadn't seen Horace. The bump was too much to add to Horace's frenzy. He interpreted it as an attack. He shoved the man, who nearly fell. This event prompted the man to raise his cane and grumble at Horace. This more direct threat was, for Horace, a declaration of war. Nearby, some sewer workers were working on an underground problem. At that moment, they were taking a break, leaning on the temporary guardrails protecting the open manhole. Horace had already noticed them and had misinterpreted their break as a means of monitoring him. He grabbed the elderly man and hoisted him into the air. Through traffic, Horace bounded over to the manhole, past the startled sewer workers. Horace dropped the man down into the sewer, feet first. Amazingly, the man survived, although he was seriously injured. Although his victim's luck and medical care prevented Horace from being a murderer, I worry that his release from prison will eventually bring that to pass.

One might think that Horace only wanted to be left alone, that if our complex, interconnected world would allow him to make a living and attend to his needs in isolation, then he would be happy. He would agree to this proposition, but I do not. Despite his violent overinterpretation of all human activity as threatening, Horace craved human contact. However, it needed to be highly structured and organized, protected yet adversarial. Horace has found the perfect means to gain such contact . . . in the courtroom. For the last five years, Horace has fought each attempt to hospitalize or treat him for his chronic paranoia in court. He has been partially successful in avoiding direct treatment, but in the process of this avoidance, he has formed relationships with evaluating psychiatrists, attorneys, and even judges. Indeed, he claimed that he hated the legal system, but he made many efforts to obtain often unnecessary reviews and repeat appearances. In court, he smiled at the increased contact, legalistic though it was. Only after a number of years was it discovered that Horace was making phone calls to female court personnel, entreating them to join in violent sexual activity.

Although Horace would not discuss his fantasies, his tape recordings indicated that sexuality has been intrinsically linked to violence for him. I suspect that this link has afforded him a sense of control and distance from intimacy. It may also have been a reprise of a possibly abusive past. Unfortunately, some victims of violent sexual abuse learn to link the two. It is more common for this trend to lead to repeat victimization, but a few victims go on to become perpetrators.

There are reasons that the sexuality of violence is generally ignored. The first is the noble cause of the protection of the rights and dignity of the usually female victims of rape. As mentioned before, for years, the defense of the rapist has consisted of characterizing the victims as sexually enticing and "loose." In recent years, there has been an attempt to decrease the tendency for courts to view rape as nearly consensual intercourse by portraying it as violent and not centrally sexual. Although I agree with the goal of reducing the concept that rape is ever deserved, my observation of rapists leads me to believe that rape is often sexual and violent; in short, it is profoundly perverse. Unfortunately, such profundity is not rare. Sadism is a common theme in movies, in which scantily clad women and more rarely, men, squirm in ropes and bonds. Often, it is not the protagonist who is the sadist; nevertheless, the audience can be the voyeur for such behavior. My hunch is that societal values do play a fairly direct role in violence, especially in those ill-equipped to question such values.

The sexual side of violence needs to be explored, because a greater understanding of it may aid in the reduction of murder. A fuller understanding of sadism may bring about a better plan for the prevention of its most frightening enactment, homicide.

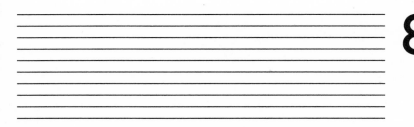

8

Late at Night

*T*HE FRONT DOOR *opened easily; it wasn't locked. It never was locked for many years—so easy to open, but no one seemed to come in. That was the paradox. Anyone could have opened that door and seen with their own eyes. They could have seen the expression on my face, and they would have been outraged. Mother called my expression "hollow" when I was scared. But every time the door opened, it was only Mother or Dad. It was never opened by anyone who would break the silence. There was no one to break the screaming.*

That night, everything seemed to be in its place. The long hallway was lit from below with a dim, plug-in night lamp. At the end of the hall, the old desk looked tired, holding up the telephone and the stack of unopened mail. Mother always was impatient and opened her mail quickly, sometimes ripping the envelope so hard that the contents would be torn or thrown onto the floor. Dad waited; he opened the mail when he was ready to read it.

Around the corner, lit by only the outside light shining through the window, the kitchen was messy as usual. Although everything was where it should be, an oddness permeated the house. It was a strange air, as though emotion had taken form in a charged mist, caught up in the pressure of retribution.

Mother and Dad would both be sleeping, each in their separate rooms. They had taken the rooms several years after the last of the children had moved out. Mother had taken my room, eliminating me from the house. She threw my stuff in a box, and when I didn't

pick it up, she shipped it to me. She had edited out
what wasn't important. Tonight, I would be reclaiming
my room.

The stairs are long, but climbed easily and silently.
The silence seemed strange, since this house held memories of my parents screaming at each other. Each
episode floated back into my mind, one for each step.

On the first step, a memory came from a long time
before. I was about ten, and it was early spring. It was
unseasonably cold that day. Mother left in the early afternoon "to go to the store," a frequently used euphemism
for leaving the house to get drunk. Dad came home from
work early and starting cutting the grass. Early in the
afternoon, our old lawnmower caught fire. By the time
Mother came home, Dad had cleaned up the wreckage.
He did the best he could with the lawn, but there was a
big black spot where the fire scalded the grass. Mother,
drunk as expected, flew into a rage. At the height of her
anger, she threw a pan at Dad. Thankfully, she missed,
breaking a lamp instead. The next morning, the mess
was tidied up and nothing more was said.

A few months later, after some similar evenings,
Dad left for three weeks. Mother was awful. She blamed
Lisa and me, scolded us, and spanked us for not making dinner. One Saturday while Dad was gone, Mother
sent us to our friends overnight. Lisa and I snuck back
and looked in the window. She was with another man.
He was younger than Dad, handsome and smiling.
That night, I could almost forgive her because she was
a knockout. She was dressed in a shiny party dress,
low-cut and shapely. She was even graceful, almost
floating. That night, she seemed younger. But the next
day, she was worse than usual, hung over. She wondered, I thought, about the curious expressions on our
faces. I looked all over that house for evidence of the
man, even though I had seen him there. I looked for evidence that they had slept together. I didn't know what to

look for. A few days later, Dad came back. I thought that a part of the woman that I had seen that night might return, but it never did. She just drank more, yelled at Dad, and spanked us more. She never told Dad about the man, and we were too frightened to tell him. Lisa and I decided that she was only good for the three S's: screaming, spanking, and sipping.

The stairs seemed to last forever, a memory for each step. Each memory was worse than the one before. Each step worsened the strange feeling of impassive dread. Each memory slowed me. Each one made my thoughts and motions heavier, thick. Yet, trudging, I kept climbing, my feet growing heavier with each step, heavy with dread. At the summit, the worst memory came. Completely forgotten the step before, as my foot landed on the second floor, the memory awoke in vivid colors and sounds. It was a day at a carnival. The sun was bright. The grass seemed so green that it held my attention for a few moments. I recalled wondering if it always looked that way and I hadn't noticed. But at eleven or twelve years old such a thought was soon replaced by the attractions of the carnival. There was the jangle of the carnival music, overtaken by the great whoosh of the oscillating rides, always followed by squeals of excited fright. On that day, the carnival seemed to stretch to the horizon. I hardly noticed that Mother was in her doldrums. She was dressed in a bright spring dress, but her eyes were cold. She held her body limply, wincing when the children screamed in high-pitched anticipation on the ride. She decided to give Lisa and me money, and let us meet her back at a bench where she could suffer alone. Lisa and I were excited, running from one stand to the next to survey everything before we chose exactly the most enjoyable way to spread out the money. Somehow, in the excitement, we lost the five dollar bill. We didn't even know who had last held it. We tried to find ways of entertaining ourselves, so we didn't appear back too soon at the bench to undergo questioning. Yet our lack of a sense of time and our guilty faces betrayed us, and Mother began asking. We broke down in the lie, and Mother began a ruthless inquiry into who had lost the money. We didn't know, we implored. She insistently questioned each of us about the other. She tried to make Lisa and me accuse each other, the choices being only blaming the other or being beaten. Knowing that, as the eldest, Lisa would get the blame if no culprit was found, I confessed to losing the money. I was proud of my courageousness, which shrank as I received what felt like a double beating for not admitting sooner. She beat me right by that bench, on the promenade of the park, in full view of the carnival. I remained quiet save for yelps, but inside I screamed my hatred. I felt it anew, standing in the darkness at the top of the steps.

Down the hallway, on the left. In my old room, my mother would be sleeping, maybe drunk. For a moment, the door seemed to be locked. But I smiled as I recalled that the lock had been broken years ago. It was amazing how hard it was to push open over the thick carpet.

Inside, the light seemed almost bright compared to the stairs. The moon was full and shining through the window. In the soft light, she seemed younger. She was nude, and the covers were strewn about, covering little. She was how I imagined her on the night that the other man came. There was something soft about her. . . . But no, the bottle was on the dresser, and her face, even in sleep, was sour. With a gulp, and straining my will, I silently said, "She deserves this."

I reached inside my coat and pulled out the knife. It was an old knife that Dad had given me as a boy. I thought that I had lost it long ago but there it was inside my jacket, strong and ready. It seemed to have a mind of its own. It danced in the pale light, shimmering. Then I pulled it down, straining against the inexplicable inertia. It was an arc of silver above this woman, my mother. I pulled it down further, toward her neck. Less than an inch from her skin, it was almost as if I could not push it any further. I seemed to try, and as always, I awakened.

This dream is fictional but similar to many dreams or fantasies about homicide. The "victim" in the dream is alive. She is the mother of the "killer," who is a fairly well-adjusted businessman. His name could be Will. Both he and his sister, Lisa, are engaged in psychotherapy related to their difficult family life as children with a somewhat passive and frequently traveling father and their angry, alcoholic, and abusive mother. The psychotherapy has helped him, but it has involved a detailed examination of his childhood. As if often the case, he has had an increase in thoughts, memories, and even feelings from that time. Beliefs that were incorporated then have been challenged, and he is looking anew at the events of the past and their meaning. Will has never threatened his mother and when awake, he does not wish to kill her. He is unlikely to be violent. If you met him, you would probably find him to be pleasant and nonthreatening. But how far away is that line of violence, even for someone relatively "normal" like Will? What if he turned to liquor instead of professional help? What if he were disabled and still dependent on his family? What if he still lived in that house? What if his mother were worse, perhaps disabled herself and now dependent on Will to care for her, all the while drinking and hurling insults?

Although Will is not a murderer, he dreams about murder. Indeed, many people fantasize about violence. Perhaps all of us do. Although the media seems to numb us with a constant barrage of homicide, we are deeply troubled by real violence. Both books and television often portray murderers as otherworldly, cold plotters bent on destruction, or wildly insane maniacs, who have a completely enigmatic yet incessant drive to kill. My work brought me to the realization that, often, all that separates us from the murderer is the line between dream or fantasy and reality. The themes in Will's dream often appear in our dreams, and often appear in the lives of murderers. People who experience a very unexpected event often report an experience of unreality, as if they are experiencing something, but it is either that they are not quite there or it is all not real—perhaps a dream. Such feelings are reported as occurring during a tragedy such as a sudden death in the family or a natural disaster, but also with a sudden positive event such as winning an award or prize, or being reunited with a lost relative. Murderers report similar feelings. When I started this work, I felt comfortable that the line between fantasy and reality was a fairly clear one, that no one I knew in my own life was capable of anything like the things done by the people that I saw in my job. But that line wavered, moved, and, at times, seemed to disappear.

9

The Victim Is the Perpetrator

THE SEXUAL and abuse-related aspects of violence are most honestly and vividly revealed by murderers and rapists who are cognitively disabled. Altemus was a forty-year-old man who sweetly greeted any visitor or staff person at the door of his secure residential facility. His kindness lasted beyond an initial greeting; he would gladly provide a tour for any visitor. Over time, his politeness could wear on the frequent visitor or employee of the facility because it felt ingenuine. He had the bearing of an inelegant politician, clumsily trying too hard at social graces. He had too wide a smile, too diplomatic a stance.

Altemus was a thin man who moved with a lightness like floating. He had been born with cognitive deficits. Although his mother was also developmentally disabled, the family teased him for being "slow." His older brother called him "the village idiot." Whenever he failed to perform his chores, his mother, father, or older brother would beat him with a belt or stick. As Altemus grew older, he managed to find ways of making sure that his chores were done, such as drawing a picture of a broom on the appointed day on the calendar for sweeping. Rather than being delighted with Altemus's ingenuity, the family became angry with the loss of "sport" they found in punishing Altemus. They began making it impossible for Altemus to complete his chores. His brother hid the broom; his mother didn't buy any dish soap. They then beat Altemus, often three against one, although Altemus never fought back. Perhaps this cruel, degrading ritual gave Altemus his

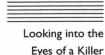

caricatured humility or the overzealous sense of duty to please the insatiable requirements of his sad, mean-hearted family.

Altemus had another possible source of his obsequious behavior. It might have been the result of an attempt to live down his dark side. This side would appear briefly and rarely, but it was strong indeed. He did not get aroused very often. When he had sexual thoughts on his mind, he would avoid contact with the clinicians. Once engaged in conversation, he would sit, quieter than usual. He would appear a bit distant, almost in a light trance. He would try the old smile, but it had even less conviction than usual. Eventually, he would discuss what was on his mind. He would begin politely as usual. "You know that new lady who works next door? She seems nice. . . ." His voice would trail off; he hoped the inquiry would stop. If it did not, he would continue with a description of the woman, her manner, then her body. He would become lewd but not disturbing until he finally admitted that he wanted to hit the woman, or burn her. When asked why, he would shrug and smile, although we all suspected that he regarded his mother as the one who led the family beatings. His charged love–hatred had outlived her and passed on to a series of women.

His mother and father had died in a car crash, and his brother followed soon after by dying in combat in Vietnam. Altemus had been placed in a large institution for the mentally retarded. For many years, a large number of people with developmental disabilities lived in these often vast, hospital-like complexes. The institutions varied in quality; some were reasonably kind places, others were turbulent and punitive. These institutions have almost disappeared as advocates for the disabled have argued that developmental disability is not a good reason for institutionalization. In most cases, the advocates are right. Many such disabled citizens live far freer and more productive lives than the superintendents of these institutions would have dreamed possible. Yet for the developmentally disabled men and women who also have behavior problems, the deinstitutionalization has been a mixed blessing. They have more freedom and can receive treatment without the high level of restriction of the old state buildings. But the small minority with severe impulses may have more access to act on them. Altemus was placed in a small group home set up by the state. His meals and furniture were provided; his days were his own. The home was about ten miles from the local beach. Altemus had grown up on the inland side of the state. The beach was a novelty; he soon mastered the bus system and traveled there nearly daily. During the fall and winter, these trips represented solace and quiet. Altemus would walk by the water and wonder what was on the other side of the ocean. By late afternoon, he would catch the bus and go back to the group home. The home keepers and other residents were pleased; Altemus displayed his trademark manners and submissiveness. He did well until late spring, when the tourists began to arrive. Women began to appear, and Altemus began to have violent fantasies. At first, he kept his behavior in check. By early summer, however, he had started touching women's bodies under the water. One woman slapped him, but most thought that he had accidentally bumped into them. When Altemus became more aggressive and slapped a young woman, she filed charges. However, the proceedings were dismissed, partially because the victim had been vacationing and lived at a great distance.

One day, Altemus was a bit bored at the beach. It was a sweltering, midsummer day. Even the wind off the ocean wasn't enough to keep cool. Altemus walked farther than usual, trying to find someplace where he could keep cool. He saw a building with glass doors and recalled how such doors often held air-conditioned rooms inside. He was also attracted by the steady stream of young women moving in and out of the building. Altemus's reading skills were poor, so he did not stop to read that the building was a tourist house for young women. Inside, he was relieved to find the lobby air-conditioned, but it was not where the women were congregating. He followed a few women out a back door, again not stopping to read signs. One woman in a bathing suit caught his eye, and he followed her until he lost her behind a flimsy partial wall made of boards. He wasn't sure whether to go right or left. In the meantime, the sound of giggling came through the wall. Altemus found that he could see through the wall if he looked at an angle, so that his vision cut through the seam between the wooden boards. Inside, about three young women were showering and splashing each other. The sight of their naked bodies and the sound of their screams overwhelmed him. He ran around the wall and began splashing and slapping the women. At first, no one came to their rescue, because they had been noisy before he came into the open-air shower room. One of the young women screamed louder, and another kicked Altemus. He grabbed the woman closest to him and rammed her head up against the wall, hard. She later died. After two years of court proceedings, Altemus was back in an institution.

Although everyone working with Altemus would learn to know his particular set of fantasies, they were shocking nonetheless. Perhaps it was Altemus's seeming inability to provide us with even a euphemism or a shallow dodge. As much as forensic psychiatrists pride themselves on the detection of malingering, the depth of thirst for blood can cause a quiver in even the most steady and experienced of hearts. Another source of trepidation was the fact that Altemus would soon revert to his usual self, smiling and greeting everyone as if nothing had happened.

Like Altemus, Lon had a developmental disability, the condition also called mental retardation. He did not share Altemus's distinct set of problems. Lon had been physically and sexually assaultive to both men and women in such a confusing pattern that there seemed to be no pattern at all. He would threaten either men or women, either young or old, with either sex or aggression. At other times, he would be quiet and calm for even months at a time. The clinical staff was desperate; they knew of no way to help Lon. In their desperation, the staff begged me to discover a cure, quite a rarity in psychiatry. Their hope for a cure of a chronic condition is a common wish among those uneducated in psychiatry. The staff knew that most forms of mental illness, and almost all forms of mental retardation, have no known cure (although symptomatic treatment can be effective). Their wish was a fantasy based on the sense of mystery engendered by Lon's problems and their feelings of powerlessness and fear. The attacks appeared in a random fashion, then suddenly disappeared. Couldn't I make them disappear and never come back?

Actually, I had trouble even conceptualizing the problem, since most patients' violence has some recognizable pattern, motive, or cycle. At first, I found no clues for this mystery. Lon himself was talkative but not about his violence. He would fill the conversation with self-deprecating remarks. He was a man in his early forties, who looked a few years older. His thinning hair was always messy, and he carried himself with a demeanor that always suggested that he had just crawled out of bed. Yet there was a trace of cunning attractiveness about him.

Slowly, some information presented itself. He seemed to exhibit the phenomenon of disinhibition, sometimes seen in patients with brain difficulties. One way of conceptualizing behavior is that it is constantly caught in a balance of opposing forces, for and against.

Each person has many more potential behaviors than actually occur, because we have (to use the vernacular) "second thoughts." Those individuals who have difficulty inhibiting behavior often get into trouble—imagine if you acted on every wild thought. Unfortunately, head injuries often involve the part of the brain thought to be instrumental in inhibition, so there are many patients with the disinhibition problem. Alcohol makes the problem much worse. A good model of this phenomenon is the behavior of a college student after the first beer or two. Lon often became loud and boisterous. He did not seem able to stop enacting the thoughts that came into his head. Yet I was still puzzled by the source of his thoughts. Rather than a specific pattern of aggressive fantasy like Altemus, Lon's behavior seemed to be random. At first, it also seemed socially disconnected. He didn't seem to have distinct enemies, and he frequently apologized for his assaults. The apologies were also interesting, since they were unusually convincing, considering how little time it would take for the behavior to be repeated. Lon clearly had difficulties with impulse control. Acting on impulse may be a frequent difficulty in patients with developmental disabilities (and others), although it is quite rare for the behavior of such patients to reach the degree of difficulty seen in Lon. It seemed that any assaultive thought that came into Lon's mind had few obstacles to fruition, yet he did not assault frequently. Maybe Lon did not think about assault very much.

The lack of second thoughts seemed clear, but there still was something missing. Even impulses often have a source. For example, people may regret those items they purchased on impulse, but there was something they liked about them. Assaults are often linked to power, fear, sex, money—something. Each of Lon's assaults had some thread of a reason, but they were disconnected. Although the phrase "random violence" is popular, the randomness is usually from the viewpoint of the victim or the media. Although not all violence is cold and calculated, it isn't often truly random either.

As Lon's behavior moderated in response to a type of medication sometimes helpful in patients with difficulties with impulse control, a frightening pattern became evident to explain the mystery.

Lon was housed in a unit in a prison for inmates with special needs. Because the staffing pattern on the unit was higher than the usual prison section, the inmates were allowed more contact with each other and with staff. Lon, though seeming to be distant and unaware, actually paid close attention to the conversation of everyone in the unit. The prisoners and most of the staff were male. Separated from contact with women, much of the conversation consisted of lewd remarks about women or rumors about homosexual contact between men. Anger was often expressed with violent threats, although many were hollow in intention. The less-well-trained staff, some of whom had known the inmates before their incarceration, would engage in what seemed like a nonstop dialogue of profane sexual fantasies and violent threats. For visiting professional staff, such talk can become like a loud steady noise in a factory—unconsciously acknowledged but essentially unheard.

Lon was listening intently, taking this idle, profane chatter quite seriously and remembering it. He became the enactor of the veiled intentions and empty bravado of the rest of the unit, mercilessly punching men and making awful, lewd advances at women. Each of the attacks was a direct response to others' conversations on the unit. Lon was like a reluctant arm forced to take orders from a violent brain. The sad thing was that the brain was not his own, but those of the other patients and staff.

Lon's case caused me to listen more attentively to prison talk. For a person visiting, it might seem profane but colorful. Listening more closely, it becomes more disturbing. In prison, everything has a consequence. If a prisoner acts improperly, a disciplinary action is instituted (such as solitary confinement). Sadly, there is a similar pattern with the officers. There is an elaborate written code for officer behavior, which is generally ignored by the officers and administrators alike until something happens. Then, to use the language, someone has to hang. An investigation ensues, a violation is found, a person is blamed. Officers frequently suspect the identified party was named for other reasons, and they may be right.

This scenario leaves the officers and the inmates in a remarkably similar situation. It is a world in which the worst crime is to tell the authorities, to be a "snitch." Each person is either your friend or your enemy, trustworthy or not. Every occurrence has a story to be told, but the one told to the investigator may be carefully planned. It is a world of unwritten rules and a structure of power and sex as payment or obeisance. Profanity is so common, so usual as a part of each sentence that it becomes meaningless. I recall joking that saying "I love you" would be far more shocking.

Sadly, I was far from the first to have discovered Lon's secret. A few of the staff, separated only from the inmates by not having been caught, had taken directly to urging Lon to act out various sick scenarios. At first, they asked him to perform various bizarre, seemingly innocuous acts such as making strange faces and walking in an awkward caricature of a woman. They may not have realized that their antics formed part of the reason that Lon's previous psychiatrist probably erroneously thought that Lon was psychotic, causing him to be treated with medication that resulted in perturbing side effects. As if this course of events was not enough, they escalated the antics. I suspect that they found out that Lon would, at their urging, act like the characters on television or in newspaper photographs. Such an observation led to a desire for experimentation, and on one evening, Lon was given some lewd photographs, which he promptly acted out. The offending staff members were fired.

Frighteningly, Lon's case may be an extreme example of a larger phenomenon. Some cognitively handicapped people have less ability to consider options when confronted with sexual or aggressive stimuli. However, the pairing of these two urges, and the enactment of such impulses, is not just a biological event. Such patients may enact the perversions that they are taught.

I would like to say that my unraveling of Lon's mystery led to a total cure. His behavior did improve, and my education of the clinical staff led to at least a moderation of his use as something like a marionette. But the power of a physician in a correctional setting is limited. I strongly suspected that, especially at night, such antics still occurred. Talking to Lon about what was happening helped more than I thought that it might; he was able to learn to distance himself a little bit. I remain sad about Lon, despite what seems intellectually to be good treatment. Even after the discovery and improvement, he would still get into trouble at times. Despite my efforts, he would often be blamed and cajoled by the nonclinical staff. This inappropriate and unstoppable blaming felt almost physically painful to me, as I found no way to stop this cruelty.

Perhaps Lon offered a striking view into the depths of the environment in which he lived. As dangerous and lewd as he was, little of it came from within him. He was the harsh mirror of what lay hidden just beneath the surface of the place, and it was dark indeed.

10

You Can Never Go Home

A COLLEAGUE told me a story about a young correctional officer who had just graduated from his training. He started work at the most secure prison in the area. At that time, he was in his late twenties. In high school, he had been a star baseball pitcher on his way to a great senior year when a shoulder injury sidelined him. He was never sure whether the injury limited his later progress or if he was never as good as he had hoped. His dream of becoming a major-league pitcher ended in a dismal season on a dusty minor league field in Texas. He came back home and drifted from job to job. Eventually, he decided to become a police officer, but he couldn't pass the entrance examination. He hadn't planned on working in a prison, but he passed the correctional officers' exam and was relieved to have found a steady job.

The night before his first day, he tried to calm himself down. He had never even visited a prison before the officer training school, and it seemed like a strange, isolated, and enclosed world, filled with dangerous inmates and experienced, gruff old guards. In his insecurity, he figured that the old-timers would try to find fault with him. He became determined to take control from the beginning and not let go. As expected, the assignment officer teased him about being new. He also gave him a hard time about his fresh military-style haircut. The new officer feigned some disappointment when he was assigned to a tier of prisoners that was described to him as relatively quiet. He wanted the old sergeant to consider him tough, but inside he was

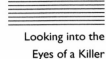

relieved. Small riots had occurred in the prison before, as had murders.

The first two hours of the shift passed without incident. As advertised, the prisoners were fairly quiet. The officers from the previous shifts had taken shortcuts in their paperwork; it wouldn't be hard to look good by making better notation of the inmates' activities. After a couple more hours, the new officer began to notice that, as warned, he was becoming bored. His classmates in the training school had told him about boredom. In prisons, the officers have tremendous responsibility. They have to watch and preside over often large numbers of people who are crimianls. The rookie officer knew about the strict rules and sensed the tougher unwritten code. The officers have to look out for each other, or the prisoners could take over, as has happened in notable instances in Attica and elsewhere. However, when all is going well, the officer's job is to count, to search, to accompany, but mostly to watch. Anyone who has served in the military can attest to the boredom of a quiet watch duty; correctional officers do it day after day. Coping with boredom is perhaps the most difficult task of the job. The pent-up energy that some of the officers collect in response to the long, quiet hours may explain their sometimes overzealous responses when something dangerous happens. The ever-possible danger lies in the shadow of the boredom. The officer can't sleep, or even fade too much, because many eyes are watching.

By the fifth hour of his first eight-hour shift, the new officer's own boredom was dissipating. He began to notice the patterns of conversation on the tier. Much of the conversation was directed to Avi, a stocky drug dealer who came to the prison after he had murdered a rival dealer. The inmates would complain to Avi about other inmates; Avi would either dismiss the complaint or issue a reprimand. Over time, the officer heard Avi issue some threats. "Cool your s---, Julio, or you will get yours." At first, this banter didn't bother the officer: He had heard about prison politics. But as it continued, he progressively became convinced that Avi ran the tier. He started paging through the logbooks for previous officers' notes about Avi. He found notation of a number of minor assaults. Then, he found many notes about two more serious incidents. In the first, Avi was found standing over another inmate with a long, handmade knife—what the prisoners call a "shank" or "shiv." In the second incident, a man was stabbed in the abdomen and had to be rushed to the hospital. He survived, but only after surgery and prolonged hospitalization. Avi was not accused of the "hit," but was thought to have arranged it. The evidence was not conclusive, so no additional charges were filed.

As the officer read the reports, he closely listened to the inmates treat Avi with respect. His blood began to boil as he realized the exalted position this violent drug dealer had arranged in prison. To the officer, it made a mockery of the courts and the law for a prisoner to be a king, even if it was king of a cellblock. As these thoughts simmered in his brain, it became the appointed time for him to walk past all of the cells for an inspection. He lingered at Avi's cell to peer in. The cell was a mess. The walls were filled with posters and the window was covered with a curtain, a clear violation of prison regulations. Avi wore a bright sport shirt over his prison garb, another violation. Also, he had more food than was allowed. Worst of all, Avi sat in the middle of his messy cell looking at the officer with a contemptuous grin. He let go of a little chuckle, and said, "Who let you in the tier, and where did you get that buzzcut?" Although the officer didn't find the statement to be funny, the other inmates obediently laughed. As he stared at Avi, he remembered his morning promise to get in control and stay there. He

immediately began to bark orders to Avi. Although he muttered profanities under his breath, Avi slowly complied. The officer kept the heat on for the next few hours, often stopping and lingering at Avi's cell to make sure that all violations were rectified. By the end of the shift, he even noticed that the inmates were talking to Avi a little less.

As the officer left the prison for home, he was satisfied with his day's performance. He felt that he had put Avi in his place. He had a smile on his face as he pulled into his driveway. He locked his truck and started up the walk to the house. He felt a light brush or tap on his shoulder but thought it perhaps an insect or bug and brushed it away. The next tap was more forceful, almost painful. He reared around to see two large men with sunglasses. One leaned forward and whispered, "Take it easy on Avi." After a pause and a smile that revealed a golden tooth, he said, "We know where you live." The next morning, his second day at the prison, the officer heeded the man's advice.

I was never threatened or accosted at home in that way, and yet my work with criminals changed my life outside of work in many ways. At first, I thought it was just a matter of safety. Seeing murderers so often makes murder very real. Some patients became and stayed angry at me, and they could be released at some point. After all, the fact that repeated murder is rare is faint emotional protection from the recognition that work with murderers invariably results in many of them becoming angry. They were probably angry when they murdered, and they have done it once. Unlisted phone numbers are minimally protective in today's communicative world; the mail-order magazine contests seem to know your whereabouts within two weeks of a move. Safety was definitely part of the issue, but another word began to burn into my consciousness during my work with this population. The word was *sanctity*. Although I had always known that people could be dangerous, it never had seemed so common or easy. Suddenly, murder seemed to loom everywhere. But it wasn't just death. I began to notice the shreds of dishonesty and deceit in everyday life that I had glossed over.

One night, an event from years before came back to me. In college, I made friends with Ward, who had graduated a year before and was working at an advertising agency. We became fast friends. I invited him to the college parties, and he brought me to the slightly more sophisticated gatherings of the young professionals. One evening, over a few beers, he admitted that he wanted to come up with a good idea for a new client. He told me about the product, and I thought of a few ideas. One of them was particularly good, and we developed it over an hour or two that evening. I subsequently began spending much of my time with a young woman I had met, so I didn't really mind that Ward hadn't returned a few calls. Then, in a magazine, I noticed that Ward and the agency had used my idea in a new promotion for the product that Ward and I had discussed. At the time, I made many excuses for Ward's failure even to thank me. I even convinced myself that he had forgotten that I had helped him. When I thought about it later, the realization that Ward knew and that it was wrong was no comfort.

I had begun to see the minor evils in everyday, noncriminal life. At a conference, a young colleague made a poignant and reasonable criticism of an ambitious professor's research. Obviously annoyed that a more junior researcher saw his own weaknesses, the professor condemned him for his failure to read an obscure and, at most, tangentially related article in the Scandinavian literature. The younger man frowned but sat back in his chair and kept quiet.

At a dinner party, I noticed a young wife's frustration with the conversational efforts of her husband, who had difficulties with public speaking, even at an informal gathering. As I silently watched the hostess's annoyance grow, I noticed another young man leading a spirited conversation nearby. I had met the man at a previous party; he had subsequently proved to be an ambitious and ingenuine salesman. After a moment, I realized that the hostess was looking longingly at the well-spoken salesman.

It was not that I had never seen these things before. In the past, they were noticed and dismissed, they never had seemed to dominate life so much. Suddenly, they seemed frighteningly present. I noticed the anger in people's faces on the road, the shoving in the subway, the soundless curses of the professional athletes when viewed close up on television. The normal aggression in everyday life took on a horrible twist, as it seemed much closer to the aggressive feelings of the murderers I was investigating.

Worst of all, my efforts at communicating my feelings on this issue with those who had not worked with criminals were frustrating. My descriptions were met with platitudes from my friends, comfortable in their nominally secure urban apartment buildings. They made remarks such as, "Well, what did you expect after working with such people," or "That's what makes the world go around." I didn't quite become depressed in the clinical sense, but I felt alone, and my soul hurt.

Over time, these thoughts became less painful, although I am still observant of the aggression inherent in so-called polite professional life. In my work with violent patients, I had become weary of the apparently unending well of murderous aggression. Horrified, I had run back to the rest of society hoping for comfort. Instead, I found that the rest of us had blood on our lips, too.

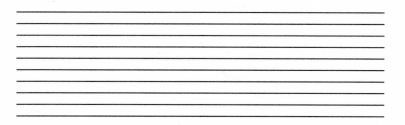

11

When the Plot
Is the Illness

AT ONE OF the earliest stages of the development of a formal insanity defense in England, in 1724, the defendant was felt to be innocent by reason of insanity if he or she acted with the drive of a wild beast. Although later legal standards have become more subtle (and far less descriptive), a series of standards, starting in 1844 and used at least until 1972, included the concept that a person is only legally insane if the drive to commit the crime was an "irresistible impulse." The actual intent of these standards was broader than the literal interpretation of this phrase, but it was that phrase that was often used. This idea is still a part of many standards, and forms the commonsense notion of insanity that many judges and attorneys use. I consider these standards, or at least the literal interpretation of them, to be based on what I term the "marionette fantasy" of mental illness—the idea that schizophrenia or other disorders are god-like, taking control of the patient from above. The idea has more than zero merit; indeed, some patients hear seemingly foreign voices telling them what to do. One elderly man that I met was called "successfully treated" by his psychiatrist because the medication had taken away the voices. Unfortunately, the patient was bored; he was angry at the psychiatrist because he missed the voices' company!

A more vexing problem both clinically and legally concerns multiple personality disorder, made famous by a number of books and films. A person with this diagnosis has a number of relatively distinct personalities that alternately take control of his or her body, making the patient's behavior seemingly unrecogniz-able from one moment to the next. For many years, this dramatic condition was thought to be quite rare, but there is a growing group of clinicians that believes it is more common. Many forensic psychiatrists are skeptical. Some legal cases have come to trial in which the patient was on the stand, blaming the crime on the "other" one inside. One judge felt it necessary to have each personality sworn in separately. I suspect that there may be more persons with variants of the disor-der than were suspected years ago, but the creativity borne of defense in the courtroom means that legal cases may give us the wrong impression. Some pa-tients have alternate personalities that act with a rela-tive lack of awareness of the others. More commonly, however, psychiatric illness distorts, exaggerates, and attenuates aspects of the patient's personality that ex-isted before the illness took hold.

For example, Maria had a set of very unusual be-liefs for years. She believed that she was the queen of a lost tribe that would only awaken if she performed sac-rifices. She heard voices of the tribe reinforcing these beliefs. Any conversation or television program that mentioned the tribes of Israel, Native American tribes, or other cultural ceremonies reinforced her delusions. She believed that *National Geographic* magazine was a holy journal that contained special messages for her alone. She spent many hours in her aunt and uncle's basement, sprawled on the floor reading old issues of the magazine and occasionally singing some odd incan-tation. Usually, her uncle would only scream for her to be quiet, but occasionally he beat her. One day, he took the whole collection of magazines and dumped them in a ravine as she looked on. She ran into the mud and tried to rescue them, but he laughed and swatted her hands until she dropped them. She was livid and cursed him. A few weeks later, she came over to her aunt and uncle's house unbeknownst to them. She snuck into the basement through a window that she had tied open. Quietly singing sacrificial incantations, she superficially cut her arms. She painted her body in a dark-blue paint and donned her aunt's wedding dress. She then ceremonially loaded her uncle's shotgun, walked upstairs, and shot him. She dragged his body onto the roof, where she painted it and performed a strange ceremony for the setting sun. She was hearing loud voices commanding her to perform these types of ceremonies for several months before the crime and for more than a year after her hospitalization in a secure psychiatric facility.

But her remarkable level of eventual recovery created a strange paradox. It allowed her to share her underlying feelings about her uncle. She realized that she had stridently hated her harsh uncle. In her efforts to explain the murder to herself, her family, and others, Maria minimized the importance of her psychosis. She noted the beatings that she had received and her uncle's destruction of her treasured magazines. She considered the murder to result from revenge and the passion of a tempestuous youth. This explanation was very convincing coming from a plainly dressed, calm woman, whose severe illness had strikingly responded to a combination of medication and psychotherapy. Many of those who had contact with her believed that Maria's insanity defense was a falsehood; they believed that she had murdered for the same passionate reasons that drive others. Some forgot the bizarre details of the murder; others decided that she had faked psychosis in dramatic detail. In my opinion, she did not fake the psychosis; her later explanation was a reconstruction of a treated woman trying to rationalize insanity. At the same time, Maria's hatred and anger were real and understandable. Her rage had a rational basis; anyone can understand the anger of a forgotten and mistreated child.

The difficulty is that the courts and the psychiatrists who attempt to help the legal system understand mental illness want the murder to be the clear product of mental illness, as if the illness has a life of its own. Although a few very psychotic patients seem so odd and unworldly that they may be unkindly thought to resemble wild beasts, most are quite, if sometimes tragically, human. The illness may distort and magnify the fantasies that the rest of us keep to ourselves. As an example, manic patients have an uncanny tendency (when ill) to drive down a thoroughfare at more than one hundred miles per hour stark naked. The rest of us attempt to confine these impulses to often nightly television and movie chase scenes and sexually provocative plots in novels.

Most vexing to some visions of mental illness is premeditation. If mental illness is pulling the strings, then certainly the marionette cannot have thought about the act before it happened (nor cover it up afterward). Yet mental illness is rarely a sudden, fulminant disease that takes a perfectly normal person by utter, sudden surprise and transforms him or her into an unrecognized maniac in an instant. Usually, the symptoms take a number of months to develop. Although psychotic patients may have grave difficulties communicating their ideas in an intelligible manner, most aspects of intelligence are preserved. There is no scientific proof (to my knowledge) that planning abilities would be expected to be universally impaired. In other words, an insane person might plan an insane act. This prospect may not seem controversial on its face, but many courts find evidence of planning to be nearly incontrovertible evidence of a lack of insanity. If Maria had ordered that shotgun and the ammunition, and if she had waited for the one day of the week when she would be alone with her uncle, would her crime seem less insane?

Part of the theoretical difficulty is the difference between rationality and reality. Patients may hold a highly delusional belief, but may nonetheless act decisively, even rationally. How can this be? Wouldn't a psychotic person behave randomly, with no direction, in utter confusion? Actually, no. Psychotic people have areas of loss of reality that generally are circumscribed. Even more severely disturbed patients often have preservation of many normal thinking functions. The vast majority of these patients, perhaps even most of those who do not take medications, function outside the hospital. Many patients, with treatment, have no symptoms at all. There is another group of patients that continue to have symptoms but function within the world. Some of this latter group are homeless and seemingly aimless. But many live relatively normal-looking lives, buying food and other needs, cleaning, and cooking. Many collect government funds, some work at jobs, and many walk unrecognized amid the larger population, even as voices and false beliefs pervade their mental lives.

Indeed, even behavior related to false beliefs can be rational in a sense. Many patients act quite rationally beyond the belief. In other words, if the false belief were true, you would do the same thing that they did. Of course, nothing in psychiatry is this simple. Isaac Ray, the forefather of forensic psychiatry, and other thinkers in the middle to late part of the nineteenth century, believed that there could be an illness that only affected morality. Those afflicted would reason well and behave normally except related to moral behavior. This idea fell into disfavor long ago. We now notice that most major forms of mental illness have many effects, but some can be quite subtle. Usually, the false beliefs extend beyond those that are immediately revealed. The patient believes the delusions to be true, so you cannot ask, "Do you have any other delusions?"

Often, delusional beliefs are accompanied by some level of fragmentation or disorganization of thinking. But even here, our assumptions are challenged. Many patients with disorganized thinking have far more organized behavior than you would think. More than a few present what seems to be a random jumble of thoughts that turns out to be an organized, if odd, labyrinthine and irrational system of thought. Unfortunately, current guidelines and funding for mental health care and evaluation usually preclude clinicians from taking the time to learn the rather intense "code" that such patients have.

Even very obsessive (and seemingly overorganized) people can become quite psychotic. Kara was a young woman who had developed a belief that the ground transmitted secret, harmful sound waves. When I first met her, her appearance revealed some worry but was otherwise normal except for her strange boots. They were large, Army-style boots that had obviously been modified. I first saw Kara on a hot summer's day, and the boots looked very uncomfortable. They were thick leather, and extended up to her mid-calf. Most striking, however, were the soles. Kara had glued an extra rubber sole on the bottom of the boots, doubling the already prodigious distance from her feet to the ground. These unwieldy devices made her gait more than lack grace. She took short, wide, clunky steps like a latter-day Frankenstein. Other than her strange boots and walk, the casual observer would find her only excessively perfectionistic unless the topic of conversation turned to the subject of her paranoia. She could speak logically and convincingly about the problems in the prison where she was housed. But the moment that the subject of the sound waves arose, the dialoguc became bizarre. She believed that the government had perfected a means of directing highly concentrated sound waves through the ground. She thought that this technology was originally developed for war, but that it had been turned upon citizens who protested against the government. Kara had grown up as the daughter of an Army colonel but had defied him in college by protesting the Vietnam War. She believed that the government was eternally punishing her for this infraction. At one point, Kara thought that moving quickly might confound the secret sound-wave technology, so she ran and drove at a rapid pace. The running made her fit but tired. At another time, she developed the idea that she might be safer if she escaped to the rugged landscape in the Rockies, reasoning that it would be harder for the military to direct the sound waves through the mountain rocks. However, the trip only served to increase her paranoia because of the presence of a number of military bases along the way. Kara began driving faster and faster. Not surprisingly, eventually a police officer stopped her. Unfortunately, the police in that jurisdiction wore brownish-green uniforms instead of blue. Kara was convinced that he was a military police officer posing as a traffic cop. He approached her window, and she smiled and appeared friendly. When he asked for her license and registration, she fumbled through her papers. She gave him her license but said that her registration was in the trunk. She politely asked if she could have a moment; she explained that the registration was among a large group of papers in a briefcase. The officer obliged her request; he returned to his patrol car to call in her license number for a routine check. This return to his car was what Kara had anticipated. She had lied; the registration was in the glove box. She went to the trunk and removed her expensive handgun. She then left the trunk lid open, as if she were still looking for the registration. She crawled along the side the patrol car. She quickly arose and shot the police officer once, fatally wounding him. She then removed him from the car. Thinking that she would better escape the government's deadly sound waves if she were disguised as an officer, she changed into the officer's clothes and sped off in the police car. In the trial, it was pointed out that the murder was deftly handled. It may not have been planned before she was stopped by the policeman, but it was not an impulse. Kara had lied to the officer about the registration, fooled him with the trunk lid, and snuck up on him. As many people would say, it didn't sound "crazy." Indeed, it does not sound as if a sudden uncontrollable urge had taken over in the instant that she killed. Most courts have officially replaced the statutes that used to define legal insanity as an "irresistible impulse." Nonetheless, in practice, many still find the idea of planning contradictory to psychosis. For Kara, however, the brooding, plotting, and planning are not evidence of her psychological health; they are the essence of her illness.

For me, she was one of the harder patients to tolerate. She demanded to sit directly across from me. During our conversation, she stared, examining me carefully. She wished to know my every thought. Insistently, she questioned the purpose and intent of all of my questions. When she inevitably came to realize that I did not believe in her delusion, she hissed contemptuously. Her long, thin face and pursed, angry, hissing lips were daunting. As each of my questions was met with louder and more vehement hisses, I hesitated to ask any more. As she shook her head and became red-faced with her viper-like hisses, I began to believe that she planned to spit at me. Rather unnerved, I ended our encounter with some haste after gathering the necessary information for my report. The untimely end to the interview enabled me to leave for home early. As I drove home on the highway, I realized that my reaction was similar to the court's. Kara's problems were not easy to endure. As a rule, I think that we picture insane murderers as wildly insanely—crazy eyes, scraggly hair, bizarre verbalizations issuing forth at loud volume. We certainly do not expect someone like Kara. She had a good vocabulary, which she used quite appropriately until she started hissing. She was always angry but in an organized way. She filed many official prison grievances. Although they annoyed the administration, they were usually correct (except when they involved the sound waves). Despite her insistent belief in a ridiculously untrue plot against her, Kara aroused no pity for being ill. Her psychosis was too organized, her criticism too sharp. The idea of her illness and plight aroused sympathy, but in the room, she was annoying.

At the time that I was evaluating Kara, my work took me on frequent, long journeys from home. That first day, driving home after talking to Kara established a pattern for a week or two. Each day, as I drove home, other thoughts would give way until I was thinking about why she was annoying. Her case troubled me. My evaluation did not involve whether Kara should be found not guilty by reason of insanity for murder. A court had already decided that she was guilty. That finding troubled me, because her illness seemed to have dominated all of her behavior. I worried that my negative feelings toward her weren't the first. What if she had annoyed the psychiatrists who had examined her for the trial? What if she was bright, strong-willed, and defiant in the courtroom? Had she been found guilty not because she wasn't insane, but because she was annoying?

These thoughts rolled over and over in my head on my way home. Thankfully, they usually stopped by the time I reached my driveway. But each afternoon, they returned. I realized that she was more than annoying. She also was challenging. It was not just difficult to sit with Kara; her case, especially her intelligence, and planning challenged our concept of insanity. After working with this realization, I grew weary of Kara and her unwanted intellectual company on the way home. As any psychiatrist would, I examined my own motives for this repetitive rumination about Kara. Although she was physically attractive, I was not highly sexually attracted to her. Although I was concerned about the verdict in her case, I did not have any designs on rescuing Kara. Rescue fantasies are a common occurrence in work with the downtrodden. Although it is good to have hopes for improvement, overzealous attempts at cures in seriously ill patients often end in disappointment. The fantasies and their enactment often more meet the needs of the practitioner to feel important. Real improvement with these patients often takes years and slow, measured work. There are rarely sudden cures and certainly no parades in work with mentally ill criminals.

My search for my reasons for thinking about Kara brought me back to . . . well, thinking about Kara. I began to recall more of her conversation and, in so doing, realized the source of my fascination. Kara was, to use the slang, in my face. She wanted to know my purpose for interviewing her. She wanted to know my assumptions, my methods, and my style of interviewing. Her questions were not only related to her interview, but she also wanted to know whether I made any departures from the routine in her interview; if so, what was usual, and why had I deviated from it? She was like the child who asks, "Why is it morning?" When answered with "Because it is early in the day," the child deftly questions, "Why is it early in the day?" The parent answers (he or she thinks cleverly), "Because the sun has just risen." At this point, it is hoped the parent expects the next question, "Why does the sun rise?" The parent is forced to try to change the subject or enter into a discussion of cosmology or astrophysics.

In a similar manner, Kara reduced our conversation down to my assumptions. More important, we reached the assumptions that formed a basis for my work, many not my own. I worked under the statutorily defined concept of insanity, an all-or-nothing concept in which a person either is or is not insane, and thus is either placed in a hospital or a prison. Yet the range of presentation of illness, and the range of motivation for violence, is limitless. Kara questioned me about my questions and caused me to think about the elusive understanding of personality. Heinz Kohut was a psychoanalyst who wrote about the in-depth treatment of patients with narcissistic problems. These people often annoy others with their selfishness and lack of care for others. Yet inside, they have a very poor self-image. The vain portrayal of themselves is a final effort; if they can convince others, maybe they can convince themselves. Kohut wrote about these patients' need for a mirror in another person, a way of seeing themselves in an appropriately positive way through the actions of another person. They don't need false affirmation that their bragging is true; they need credit for their accomplishments and reasonable criticism for their shortcomings.

Kara was like a mirror in this sense, only she was a wavy mirror, like the ones at old amusement parks. In one, you would appear grotesquely tall; the next, short and squat. Kara gave a distorted image back to me, an image of the shortcomings of my job. One of the tasks of adolescence and adulthood is adjusting to the realities of the world. As a youth, it is easy to see the way things should be. But if we demand to work under ideal circumstances, we will never work. Kara never worked. She couldn't accept the shortcomings and inconsistencies of the real world, so she constructed her own world that would survive if this devilish plot were undone, like scores of science-fiction movies. On

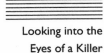
the other hand, I had hoped to change the intersection of psychiatry and the law, to make the law more mindful of the vagaries of mental illness. In the meantime, I had to function in a vague, simplistic, and punitive system that could let murderers walk and yet abuse innocent, psychotic people in prison.

Kara locked into that adolescent inside me, the one that thought that I could change the world. That adolescent felt that I had given in, had succumbed to the middle-aged world of meetings and papers, agendas and conferences. Slowly, the edge rounded off; my provisional acceptance of a corrupt system was no longer so provisional.

Kara, like me, was fascinated with theory. As an adolescent, and still as an adult, I had hoped that an understanding of theory could be liberating. If we know the reasons behind our practices, we can change them. Kara was utterly convinced and rather convincing of the inaccuracy and damaging effects of the many faulty theories of the world. For her, no theory should be used, unless it was true. In her eyes, and in the eyes of the more idealistic man inside me, our theories seemed patched and worn, taped and shredded.

Kara, a brilliant but insane woman, was found guilty and not insane, perhaps due to her style and planning, and perhaps due to the limitations of psychiatry and law. My evaluation could not reverse this error. Her interaction with me helped me to rekindle some naive idealism that, tempered by experience, helped me to work with her and the many sad others poorly served by the sometimes weak theories of psychiatry and the cold cruelty of the law. A murderer, and one of the most annoying people that I have ever met, she left me with a revitalized sense of myself.

12

The Hole

MANY INMATES call solitary confinement "the hole." It is often served in a dark room where inmates who have caused difficulty within the prison spend twenty-three hours a day; they have time outside for one hour. The room is designed to allow little possibility for danger; a simple bed or mattress sits alone near an uncovered toilet. As the most imprisoning section of prison, it is the defining part for me. Prison is a "hole," in perhaps all of the connotations of that word. Each is usually decrepit and dirty, decorated in fading paint and full of hollow sounds of doors locking and people screaming.

On a deeper, unconscious level, the term *hole* connotes the anus and toilet. Indeed, fecal and waste terms are frequently used in impassioned speeches about crime. Like the soiled waste that now pollutes many streams, we wish for these people to disappear from sight. Like soiled waste, they appear to leave, and do not.

Prisons are separated from the rest of society by elaborate security and often remote geography. These methods serve not only to keep inmates in but also to keep those other than family out. My first visit or two felt very strange. The front windows were extraordinarily straight and clean. The sunlight reflected off them, shining what felt like a spotlight on me. I felt repelled by the light but persevered. The door was heavy and hung in an unusual way, so that opening it took more force than would seem necessary. The awkwardness of this opening, combined with a slow acclimation to the relative dark inside, led me to feel out of sorts from the beginning. I reached a large, thick window with a tiny shielded porthole. Inside, there were at least two barely visible officers. One begrudgingly came to the porthole as I approached. He gave me a faint, angry smile and asked my business. His colleague joined him in checking a large sheaf of papers for the sheet authorizing my entrance. Neither found the sheet. One stared at me, then picked up the phone. The other sat down but then unexpectedly arose, looked through the stack again, and found the sheet. The man on the phone hung up and gave both his colleague and me dirty looks. At that point, I was well into the task of questioning the importance of my visit. Next, I was allowed to enter a small hallway by opening an imposing steel door with small windows. Like the outside door, it was hard to open, but this time, it at least looked heavy, so I felt a bit less awkward. At this point, the same two men could again see me through another window from their room. In this small corridor, I had to empty any metallic objects from my pockets and attempt to traverse a metal detector. It was visually identical to those in airports but much more sensitive. I could not hear whether the device detected metal or not, leading to a series of false starts for the next door. This sequence was apparently hilarious to the two men, who were joined by a third for the festivities. I was beginning to sweat. Finally, my shoes and belt removed, I passed.

I found myself on the other side of the detector, my arms full with my shoes, belt, and the contents of my pockets. I clumsily tried to put everything back together quickly, because others were waiting for their entrance. Once inside, I was relieved to find the physician who had invited me. Having hastily redressed, I tried to regain my composure. I quickly had to face another heavy door, triggered like those before by a loud buzz by the supervising officer. Once through, I tried to collect myself and began to look around. The walls were made of cinder block, painted many times, making the sharp irregularities of the concrete blocks smooth, spots of similarly pale green and yellow winking out from behind the current, stained pale brown. The interior windows, though placed in standard frames, were a series of thin planes housed in thick steel holders, like big glass and steel venetian blinds. These were designed so that an inmate would have to disfigure thick metal to climb out. Looking outside, the still-bright sun gleamed on the double row of fences and barbed wire. Inside, there was a neat but tired visiting room, with a long row of tables separating the inmates from family and friends. The furniture was worn aluminum and vinyl of a style popular in state schools and offices twenty years earlier. On the wall, separated by great distances, were dusty paintings, dark and sad, but housed in gaily painted frames, like the painted smiling mouth of a frowning clown. Noticing the focus of my attention, my host hastened to point out that they had been painted by inmates; he didn't know that I already had guessed that. The inmates' rooms were small and dark, rows of cots against bare walls. Somehow, the discipline of army barracks that I had seen elsewhere was missing, although the equipment was similar. The faces were sad, angry, and searching. Though a forgotten place for most, the visit was unforgettable. Looking back, it seems more than odd that such an inauspicious beginning would spawn a career.

I left from the same gate where I had entered. I realized that beneath my false smile to the guards, I was angry. The glaring glass, the detector without a signal, the laughing guards, the undressing—it seemed like a sick research study designed to induce frustration. Maybe I felt like a rat trying to press a bar to get out. Instead, I was shocked.

I'd like to say that my initial experience forced me to leave some of my psychological adornments at the door, that I was not so much a physician, an academic, a researcher—I was a person. Maybe there is some truth to the idea, but it is more accurate to say that I was angry, really angry.

Many days later, I learned that an officer had insulted a fragile patient. The officer was gone for the day and extremely unlikely to benefit from my instruction or advice. It wasn't big enough of an event to call the supervisor, which would have more literally made me a "rat" (equivalent to a snitch) in the officers' eyes. I felt powerless and confused, then angry.

I fantasized about revenge—not against that officer, but against those at the front door, the ones who had laughed at me. I don't recall the specifics, but in my daydream, I was in charge. I got the last laugh.

Every day, I entered through that same gate. The second day was easier than that first visit, and by the fourth, they were waving me through. Some mornings, there was one officer who said nothing. Objectively, he seemed placid, even pleasant in most ways. His body movements were controlled, fluid. But his eyes contained a meanness, a darkness. Perhaps the phrase "looking right through you" captures it. Maybe it was worse than that. It seemed like he dissected you first. I tried to ignore him, dismiss him, see a brighter side. But he always seemed to be a beacon of darkness saying, "Stay out." It was a message that I ignored daily.

Why did I keep going? I came back to such places to investigate the sources and meanings of insanity and murder. I think that this forbidden land urged in me a fascination to see the unspoken, to know what was hidden behind the walls. Hoping perhaps for simple truths, I found both evil men and terrifically forgotten souls, sometimes in the same inmate. While I hope that some understanding has resulted from my work in what can still be called the dungeons, it has been at the expense of a deep innocence that all of us try to maintain.

At Halloween time, when I was a child, there was always a building set up to be a fund-raiser as a "house of horror." People would go in, decorate, and dress up as ghosts and goblins. You paid a small fee, were scared, and then went home. The prisons embody a far more chilling form of fear. Certainly, it is the rape that occurs, the strange behavior, the histories of murder and violence. Over time, the abuse by some of the officers and the lack of insight of some of the administrators multiplied the feeling. Then, I began to believe the paranoia of prison culture. They said that anyone could be set up, meaning that the powerful could make it look like anyone had committed an error. I noticed the hushed conversations, the way that rights were abrogated, idealism extinguished, and healing banished.

I entered as part of my training, maybe fancying myself something like an archaeologist, anthropologist, or explorer. I would study, take notes, take (mental) pictures. But then, I noticed that I was writing on the stationary. I was making decisions. I was no longer a visitor. I worked there. This realization may sound rather obvious, but it was something of a shock to me. At the time of my agreement to begin the training that took me there, I knew a fair amount about the man who would be my mentor, and about the topics of study. I knew far less about the place that I would spend most of my working time. If the austere signs, the fence, the eyes of that officer, the clank of the doors, and the flickering fluorescent lights weren't enough, there was the clock. Physicians do not usually punch in on a clock. Most work too hard anyway. It was bizarre that the professional staff had one, but the guards did, so we did, too. Interestingly, we had a separate one. I don't believe in clocks to measure work, since I think that the focus of work is better placed on a topic other than time (except, perhaps, in the extreme). But I hated that clock more than that. It was loud, but there was more. It was a powerful statement that shot deep into me: You are here now, and you are ours. Realizing that I was theirs really scared me. It may sound trite, but I felt exactly like a prisoner.

The murderer is cruel to snuff out all of the possibilities for another's life, to end it prematurely. But it is not only the murderer that is cruel. The courts take the murderers and thieves and place them in the hole, hidden from the rest of us and bereft of humanity.

I am not championing easy forgiveness of a cruel criminal or coddling of violent men and women. But there is no point in maintaining a person's life without hope. In my mind, the punishment far worse than time or isolation is the lack of hope in these places, a lack that I do not believe is a deterrent to crime. In an odd mix of obeisance to the prisoners' rights movements of past decades and fiscal shortfalls, many prisons have become neither rehabilitative nor houses of strict discipline. Rather, programs decline while the televisions remain. Ironically, in some cases, television and its relentless presentation of violence may have been an impetus to the prisoners' offenses. The discipline becomes lax, punishment more unpredictable, rules sometimes so numerous as to be ruleless. There is neither the motivation of kind encouragement nor strict enforcement. That anyone leaves less likely to commit crime often seems to be only a product of lassitude, fatigue, and age.

Some time after starting this work, I visited an old jail that has since been torn down. It had more of a majestic horror, a large central room three stories high, with all the tiers of inmates and cells visible and contributing to a loud cacophony. Looming in the center of the floor were a set of translucent panes of glass. An unearthly glow came from below. The superintendent proudly told me it was the site of the gallows door many decades ago. Only slow pipe organ music was missing, replaced by the plaintive voices of men fighting, pleading, and beckoning.

13

The Mind Murderer

ALEX WAS ONLY twenty when he came to the hospital. He was serving his second sentence in the prison system. The first was for assault, the second for murder. Early in his sentence, he was gruff and cocky. He paraded around the hospital, wearing his correctional clothes like they were something he had just picked up at a suburban store. He had an air that he didn't belong. He'd flip a chair around and sit on it backwards, then wave dismissively as if he were the boss. He seemed like a streetwise version of a visiting dignitary. He told one psychiatrist that the charge resulted from a drug war in which many people were shooting. He said that he was charged and convicted because the police wanted him, because he was making too much money selling cocaine. But slowly, a change occurred in Alex. He no longer smiled and bragged. Less intrusive, he became sad and quiet. When a new psychology intern came to the prison hospital, Alex agreed to enter into psychotherapy with her. Slowly, Alex admitted that his drug dealing supported an expensive drug habit, which he said was the only way that he knew to escape endless despair. His mother, who cared for him, had died of a drug overdose when he was fifteen. He was left in the care of a successful but distant father. Slowly, Alex admitted to his therapist that his father was neglectful and unpredictably violent. He also lavished Alex with gifts, perhaps as an apology for beating him. Alex's therapist was a bright young woman who was well spoken and motivated. After her internship ended, she was hired by the prison hospital.

Her confidence and communicative abilities were noticed, and committee memberships soon evolved into a position of power. All the while, she continued to work with Alex. She championed for his continued stay at the hospital at a point when he could have been returned to prison. Many prisoners were mentally ill; the hospital services to the convicted prisoners had to be based on some priority of need, an issue that was argued over when new admissions were looming. At one point, another patient's urine sample tested positive for drugs. He claimed that Alex was the source of the drugs. An investigation showed that Alex had little contact with the patient. Nonetheless, some clinicians wondered if it would be safer for Alex to return to regular prison. They argued that he had appeared to recover from his depression, and that continuing hospitalization was not indicated. Meanwhile, in psychotherapy, Alex likened the accusations of drug dealing to the murder charge, as well as to his mother's death, something for which (he said) he had always felt responsible. His therapist felt that these issues were pivotal and argued forcefully for his continued stay.

In truth, Alex had built up a small but lucrative drug ring in the hospital. The patient who was caught had received the drugs through another patient, but Alex was the supplier. When the "snitch" returned to prison, he was beaten up, possibly as arranged by Alex. Alex's stay at the hospital provided a more comfortable place for him, as well as less competition in the drug trade. The prisons had many suppliers. Alex was the major source at the hospital.

When the facts came out, his therapist felt embarrassed and betrayed. She was very angry at Alex, and it was difficult for her to realize that not all of his stories had been lies. I believe that he did feel guilty about his mother's death. He especially regretted that he had frequently lied to his mother and told lies about her to his father. His relationship with the therapist was a reenactment of this ambivalent attachment to his mother, lies and all.

Alex demonstrated the difficulty in treating the maximally effective psychopath, who can feign emotion so well that he can enlist the help of others in his exploits. Alex was a true chameleon. He did not have a clear sense of himself inside, but he was exquisitely aware of even the most subtle alterations in others. Through this ability, he constructed his drug network and learned to understand his therapist's foibles, so that he could distort his story to his benefit. Ultimately, his ambitious plan was doomed to fail, but it was hard for everyone who had known him not to feel foolish for being duped.

I am not much of a sailor, but I have been invited to go sailing by several friends. One of the most exciting parts is when the sail has to be switched from one side of the mast to the other, a process called *coming about*. It is a dramatic moment. The sail seems to fight to stay on the one side. In a flurry of human activity, it is pulled over. It flutters with little wind in the center, then gets opened by the wind in an arc of white, and the boat is off again.

With Alex, I felt kind of like the mast. As he seemed to improve, I saw the therapist pull the staff to be his champion. I have been duped, too, but I was skeptical of Alex. I did not know specifically about the drugs, but he seemed to be a little too improved; it felt like an act. When the word was out, I saw the staff change sides like the sail. Suddenly, he was awful. A fight to keep him at the hospital turned into a fight to get him back to prison. I saw it all as Alex's repetitive drama: a good boy who deserves a treat, a bad boy who deserves a slap. I tried to point out how the staff was repeating the drama, but I wasn't heard over the sound of the changing wind.

14

The Legal Criminal

Aʟᴇx ᴄᴀᴍᴇ from a fairly wealthy household. Most people with antisocial personality disorder seem to come from poorer families. Most are not murderers, but we as a society find them to be despicable. They are often alcoholic, abusive, angry, violent, irresponsible, and dishonest. They are also survivors.

I am not making excuses or championing their cause. But there is a problem. The same society that derides the sociopath seems to honor the ruthless executive, the stylish sexual adventurer, and the athlete with the "killer" instinct.

Theresa, as a girl, was something of a tomboy. She tended to be friends with boys, and they tended to get into trouble. Theresa usually escaped blame. She was the daughter of the wealthiest merchant in a small city, and she was a girl. The parents and police blamed the boys and saw Theresa as merely being peripheral. Only her friends knew that she was the ringleader. When a warehouse was burned down, people suspected that Theresa's friends were to blame. The police investigated, but the prosecutor concluded that there was not enough evidence. But in the aftermath, people found out that Theresa was more involved than had been previously believed.

Near the end of high school, a new family moved into the city. Theresa fell in love with the new boy in town, and they were married just after graduation. Many people believed that Theresa would now revert to a life more in line with the expectations of women at that time. Theresa and her husband attended a nearby college. After graduation and the birth of her first child, Theresa returned home because her father had died suddenly. The family was expected to sell their business. Theresa convinced them to allow her to run it. Her husband went on to law school. Within several years, the business had more than tripled in size. Theresa was a prominent citizen of the city, appearing at every event in lavish clothes. She was sued on a number of occasions, but she usually won. Her husband defended her actions in court and by exercising power gained from a series of elected offices.

But the character of the business had changed. Although always successful, the business had been run differently by her father. He was modest and looked out for the town and other people. He placed his stores in profitable locations but allowed room for his competitors to thrive. He considered his employees to be like family, visited them if they were ill, and gave generous retirement benefits.

Theresa was cutthroat. She altered prices between different stores to undercut competition and put smaller companies out of business. She laid off workers whenever it suited her and threatened to move a major part of her business to another state if disgruntled workers did not quiet down. The retirement plan was gutted (she called it "streamlined"). But she gave money to charities such that her picture was in the newspaper, and she manipulated politicians through her husband, money, or the threat of lost jobs.

There were, roughly speaking, two views of Theresa in the city. One was that she was a modern success story, a person who had brought more success to her family's company and to the town. They dismissed her differences from her father as the differences between generations and the times themselves. Theresa was current, up-to-date in how business was done. The other view was that she was just like she was as a

child, burning things down. A psychiatrist seeing
Theresa would be unlikely to diagnose her as having
antisocial personality disorder. First, she was female,
and most people with antisocial personality disorder
are male. But even the many male executives with similar behavior would be unlikely to receive the diagnosis. To be fair, they probably would not meet the
criteria for the disorder as defined by the American
Psychiatric Association. In a sense, that is the problem.
The diagnosis seems to be biased against the poor and
the near-poor. I am not the only one with these thoughts,
but there is little written about it. I am not a Marxist,
but one can easily imagine the following scenario that
seems to support Marx's theories. Our society arrests
people for stealing from the wealthy, but not (as much)
the wealthy who sometimes steal legally (or close
enough). One can go on to imagine that the robber who
actually breaks through a window is labeled antisocial,
whereas the robber baron inside the house is not. I am
not hoping for Robin Hood here; the problem is that
psychiatry seems to be condoning an ugly side of Western society—the part that supports immoral activity if
it is financially successful.

Perhaps we abhor stealing and support forced ac-
quisition, abhor the burning down of a factory but support its closure as part of "downsizing." Maybe these
activities are different. My point is that there is a similarity in the people. We jail the sharks that swim in
the pool halls or local barrooms, and envy those that
cruise the boardrooms. The very characteristics that
underlie the behavior of the sociopath—failing to take
full responsibility for your actions, failing to care for
those that depend on you, taking such that others get
less—are characteristics of both. But as a society, we
revile those that do it at the stealing-and-burning level,
and admire those at the acquiring-and-downsizing one.
I may be too hard on the committees that make the

definitions of these disorders, but it almost seems that they have carefully written the criteria to make sure that the recipient of the label wears a leather jacket, not a tailored suit.

What are the implications of this oversight? On a practical level, it means that psychiatrists, possibly unintentionally, wind up endorsing society's distorted view, including in court. On a deeper level, it is the process that disturbs me. Perhaps psychiatry fails to offer an enlightened view of this topic. Perhaps we merely provide a pseudoscientific set of words and labels that reinforces the distorted societal view. One group of people we label as bad, and the others we call good people who use tough tactics. If the profession fails in this regard, the failure seems to be a particularly troubling one, for psychiatry in this regard is being the robber baron. We are, in essence, lying. We are saying, or at least, allowing that the same behavior is bad in one arena and good in another. I don't think that anyone really planned to lie in this manner, but lying under the guise of telling the truth, under a layer of legal or scientific language, is exactly the behavior of sociopaths that don't look like sociopaths and don't get called that name.

15

Remorse

ELISSA BEGAN to feel paranoid when she was sixteen. At first, her symptoms were mild. She thought that other students in school knew more about her than they let on. As time passed, however, she began to think that there was a more elaborate system of surveillance tracking her. She was able to graduate from high school, and she took a job at the local post office. There, she had a boss who spoke pedantically about the post office system and how his workers should fit into the "overall scheme" of the mail operations. Elissa thought that he smiled in a devilish manner after these comments. She began to take these beliefs quite literally and believed that the post office was engaged in a "scheme" to monitor people under any sort of suspicion from the government. For unclear reasons, she was convinced that her family was being watched. She quit her job and remained at home, often peering nervously out the window.

Her father was a jovial man who deeply loved Elissa. Her mother was more distant and depressed. Elissa began to suspect that all delivery companies were cooperating with the government in their surveillance. Her mother worked at a florist's shop and occasionally made a delivery. Elissa began to suspect that her mother was part of the plot, and that she was planning to harm the rest of the family. Elissa gravely over-interpreted statements by her mother, who said that she "didn't know what was going to happen" with the family's finances, and that they "were going down the tube." Elissa interpreted this statement as both a threat

and a reference to the long, tube-like mail-handling devices that she had seen at the post office. One needn't be Sigmund Freud to note the sexual overtones of her worry.

Although both her mother and father were concerned about Elissa's departure from her job and her sullen, worried appearance, they did not realize the depth of Elissa's psychosis. They suggested help once or twice but did not avidly pursue it. One day, Elissa's mother came home early with another employee from the store. They were carrying long boxes of hardware equipment for Elissa's father. Elissa was convinced that the boxes contained guns. As they approached the house, the neighborhood postal truck came into view in the distance. The confluence of events was too much for Elissa. She ran and grabbed her father's pistol, screaming the whole time. As her mother and the coworker entered, she shot and killed both of them. Elissa was found by the court to be not guilty by reason of insanity, and she was sent to a hospital.

At first, Elissa remained highly fearful on her unit. The hospital was state-run, and all of the paperwork and offices reminded her of the post office. She was afraid but not violent in the hospital. She reluctantly agreed to medication and slowly improved. Over time, psychotherapy was begun, eventually exploring the issues of her real anger at her mother, her attraction for her father, and her frustration with her job and family. As her paranoia abated, her grief became more evident. She began to realize that her delusions had been quite false, and that the murder was very unnecessary. Over time, she recalled the positive attributes of her mother, including her quiet kindness. Elissa had a strongly compelling level of remorse for her crime. She was active in her treatment, with faithful attendance at therapy sessions and appropriate curiosity about medication. Sitting with her was difficult at first, partially because of

the depth of her struggle. She looked to me for more
than encouragement. Elissa wanted to know why she
had become paranoid, what that meant about her as
a person. Deep down, had she meant harm to her
mother? It did not take long for both of us to realize that
I could not answer these questions for her, although
their depth was startling. Moreover, the tragedy of her
situation weighed on me. Elissa came to the hospital after what may have been a genuine attempt to protect
her home, a place she may not see for a long time. Although such hospitals are often called "secure," this
term is unidirectional. The public is relatively safe from
the patients, but the patients are not always well protected from each other. Although some staff members
think that patients' reports of rape and other assaults
represent the fantasies or delusions of patients, it
seems likely that they occur frequently. It is not easy to
treat paranoia in a house of fear. Yet despite the emotional coldness of the hospital, Elissa fashioned a tenta-
tive trust with me and opened the bolted door into her
emotions. Perhaps my understanding for her relates to
the similarity of our intellectual struggle. She had been
told by many well-meaning caretakers that the murder
was a product of her illness, and that her responsibility
was to take care of herself and continue outpatient care
when released. However, she, like me, looked deeper,
wanting to know the source of the illness, whether it
sprang just from some genetic irregularity, or whether
it was some more meaningful shortcoming or the product of a spiritual or philosophical struggle Her sad eyes
asked, "What wrong turn did I make to end up here, my
mother dead and blood on my hands?"

Psychiatrists observe a group of symptoms that
tends to cluster together and describe the condition as
a syndrome or disease. The difficulty is that some believe that the act of this observation and diagnosis ob-
viates the need for a thorough understanding of how

15 Remorse

each patient reached that place. Of course, such a search may never be complete, and one patient's woes may not be easily applied in the understanding of the next, even if the complaint is the same. Yet understanding, and perhaps even its pursuit, can form a strong therapeutic bond. Sadly, it sometimes seems easy for us to lose that therapeutic curiosity. For me, curiosity became an obsession.

Earlier in my training, I had been assigned a mentor who was a researcher. Our talks occasionally related to clinical challenges, but they eventually seemed to revolve around a single question. Can you study the "big picture"? I wanted to study the meaning of illness, the structure of psychiatry and psychological theory. I was fascinated with these issues and was convinced that they could be studied directly through theoretical analysis and clever experiments. My mentor was a reductionist, although a bright and affable one. He believed that research happened at the level of smaller, clearer questions. Eventually (so the reductionist story goes), these questions add up to bigger solutions. I thought of this kind of research as digging ever-longer and narrower tunnels. Sometimes, they did break through into a cave of insight or intersect with another tunnel. But mostly, they isolated themselves with a language that translated poorly to others, with results that often seemed only true in a tunnel (and often a specific tunnel at that). My mentor capped off his discussion by saying that investigating the big questions wasn't exactly proper. The senior researcher, nearing the end of a career of research (in a tunnel), could pontificate on larger issues. I imagined an older miner coming out from years beneath the Earth's surface to tell of the cosmos. The idea is fascinating in its paradox but was not how I wanted to plan my work.

I still think that my mentor was wrong, but he was right about at least one thing. My research career has not been direct, well trodden, or always very clear. But it has allowed me to be open to new patterns and possibilities. Unfortunately, the research establishment works exactly like the mining model. I recently was turned down for a research grant. I wanted to study the work of proponents of various theories of health and the ways that they conducted research. In this way, I felt that I might show that the tunnels rarely intersected, and that broader approaches might work. Sadly for a project designed to show the limitations of narrow, trial-and-error, empirical research, I was "graded" on how empirical my research was. The angry responses from the reviewers included reasonable criticism and concern, but they also were defensive. I had challenged the paradigm, and I was rebuked. It was a sobering way to learn more about the workings of the research system. I decided to modify the research project. The modifications were intended to act upon the constructive criticism but also represented the realization that the research needs to focus more squarely on that shift in paradigm from pure empiricism to a broader base. At times, I have been intimidated by such rebukes, but I have tried to learn the difference between thoughtful suggestions for improvement and the "tunnel protection system." I also have always kept my developing theories nearby when working in a clinical setting and have allowed patients to suddenly disprove them. Elissa's story is an excellent example.

I was fascinated by her remorse, which is a relatively unstudied commodity. It certainly relates to our ability to forgive, even though we don't know whether it relates to avoidance of future violence or not. Even shreds of remorse can be compelling to those who work with violent patients, since they are fairly rare.

There is a paradox here that Elissa's case may not fully illustrate. Remorse involves an appreciation, both cognitively and emotionally, of the wrongfulness of the act. This appreciation is hard to achieve for those acquitted by reason of insanity, who often have had to prove to the court that they did not realize the wrongfulness of the act at the time of the crime. If quite psychotic at the time of the crime, they may not have a good recollection of the events. It may be a lot to expect strong remorse from someone who has little memory of the event. Elissa is an exception, as her psychosis affected the content of her thought but not its form. Though psychotic, her thoughts and acts made some sense if you accepted her delusional notions. Other forms of psychosis more profoundly affect cognitive processing so that later, the events seem more obscure.

Remorse in prison is beset with other problems. Murder in prison is not terribly rare, and assault is fairly common. There is a complex commerce of sex, drugs, and favors in prison. To protect him- or herself, a murderer may be best advised to seem cunning, tough, and unpredictably dangerous. Such a display would be quite contradictory with a sad and supplicating show of remorse to the authorities.

Of course, our sense of forgiveness does not just relate to remorse. My understanding of Elissa may also have related to our similar questioning of psychiatry. Strong feelings can also come from deeper sources in the doctor's life. My younger brother had a hard time in school. He is very bright, but a variety of social and academic problems made life difficult for him until recently. When I first interviewed Peter, an adolescent facing two murder charges, the physical resemblance to my brother was obvious. I was not altogether surprised to find out that Peter also had academic problems; the opposite is more rare in adolescents in legal trouble. Also, his experience with the school system was similar to my brother's, and they both complained about the disdain of other students.

Thankfully (for my brother), they were also different. Peter came from a very rough, gang-ridden neighborhood. His family was sad and distant; they did not understand him, nor he they. When the teasing at school increased, he was too proud to tell his family. He also thought that they wouldn't care. Therefore, he sought solace with a group of other boys. Although they were loosely organized, they called themselves a gang. One of the group stole some money from a boy whose brother was a member of a more organized, ruthless gang. Suddenly, the fledgling gang was thrust into an unwanted war. Peter was beaten repeatedly. He bought a knife one day and told no one. When one of the rival gang members taunted him (in a minor fashion compared to previous events), Peter suddenly and brutally stabbed him. Despite his revenge, Peter remained angry. He felt that the gang would continue the violence. Also, he had not killed his adversary in the heat of battle, a failure that wounded his pride and enraged him. When he arrived home after the stabbing, his uncle was drunk. In the course of an argument that was mainly directed at his mother, his uncle belittled Peter. Without warning, Peter pulled out his knife and killed his uncle. He was numb to the event itself but felt shocked by his mother's reaction of horror and anger.

Peter's story was evocative. His life had been difficult, and he seemed to make up for the shortcomings that he perceived in himself through fantasy. He, like many teenagers, would dream that he was powerful and wealthy. For him, and perhaps for most of the children in his neighborhood, this pinnacle seemed to be most readily attained by the lawless actions of gangs and drug lords. Although his group was, at most, a minor gang in the city, he fantasized about being a fearless and wealthy urban warrior. When violence came calling, he felt obliged to protect this fantasized image.

He was not insane. He was appropriately fearful of the reprisals of the gang, but he was not paranoid. Other than his immaturity, he was apparently "psychologically intact." This idea caught me in what may be the fundamental paradox of insanity evaluations. He could not be psychologically intact. He had murdered two men, one with some provocation and the other for little apparent reason. Despite his lack of a history of psychiatric difficulty, despite his denial of hallucinations and delusions, did not the act itself prove him "crazy"? The answer, legally, is no. The courts have specific definitions of insanity, and he was far from them. Morally and psychiatrically, however, the issue gets blurrier. It is common sense that murder is a desperate act. In all but the most unusual situations, one would hope that most healthy individuals have many defenses before murder. Peter led me to wonder whether all murder is, in a sense, sickness and, unfortunately, a seemingly common malady.

Fueling my doubt was reminiscence. Peter looked like my brother. His struggles with identity were not entirely dissimilar from my brother's and perhaps not all that far from mine at that age. I recall Peter's soft voice telling how he solved a normal struggle in what I prayed was still an abnormal way. He tried to retain his pride, but there was a strong, underlying sadness. Although murder is the greatest tragedy for the victim and family of the victim, my time with Peter led me to realize the depth of tragedy it is for the murderer to live with bloodstained hands. It also reminded me that remorse is subjective. The difference between a tragedy to be forgiven and a horror to be avenged may be our frame of reference. What if Peter were female, or from a remote tribe rather than a gang? What if his culture taught him not to disclose his motivation but to be steely eyed and silent? Sadly, the distinction may depend on experience, and even race and culture.

Although my research often led me to the conclusion that it is the psychiatrist who is so often missing from equations trying to assess the diagnosis and treatment, Peter's case hit me hard. I understood him because he reminded me of my brother, and of me. I knew a bit about gangs and his culture. His words were evocative, but evocative specifically to me. It was clear to me how frighteningly true the simple phrase "Remorse is subjective" really was.

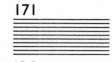

Research has suggested that white psychiatrists may diagnose black patients with more psychotic illness and may less often find their illness to be the cause of their crimes. These two findings may seem contradictory. *Psychosis* is a medical term that indicates a loss of reality such as hearing voices or believing delusions. *Insanity* is a legal term, meaning that a person is too ill to be considered guilty of a crime. It is nonetheless fascinating and troublesome that doctors of one race find people of another race to be more "crazy" (psychotic), but less "crazy" (insane). This paradox is resolved when we introduce the issue of understanding. As discussed before, insanity isn't usually random. Forensic psychiatrists look for an "insane" crime to "make sense" within the framework of the illness. They try to find the threads within the patient's history and beliefs that make the crime seem a (usually sad and tragic) part of a distorted belief system. Thus, the white doctors find the black patients to be less understandable, leading them to a diagnosis of psychosis, while that same lack of understanding prevents the doctors from linking the illness to the crime.

But there is a more sinister aspect of race relations in the Western world. White people have often been afraid of black people and found them to be bad. They have linked dark skins with dark souls. It seems likely that the lack of understanding relates to more than a lack of knowing, but a fear of knowing and a belief in some elusive difference that justifies separation. One of the saddest sides of racism in educated people is the idea that other races are completely equal, and to be respected, as long as they keep their distance. Psychiatrists call this defense projection—here, acting as if all the bad of the whites is really the province of the blacks. Sadly, identifying the phenomenon does not prevent its existence.

16

In the Face of My Own Fear

AFTER SEEING many murderers and reading about others, I sometimes worry that I have become desensitized. At one time, I frequently attended a weekly conference on the treatment of mentally ill murderers that soon began to take on a predictable course. The clinician presenting the patient's case would discuss the patient's childhood, school history, and relationships. Frequently, there was violence, alcohol, or drugs in the home. Slowly, as the clinician discussed the patient's adolescence and young adulthood, a girlfriend or mother or father's story would be woven in more and more, until it became clear that this person was the victim. At a point of tension, the clinician would pause, sigh, and say, "And then he killed her (or him)." This pattern became ingrained in my mind. One evening, although not in a sociable mood, I attended a dinner party. I was lost in my own thoughts and only half-listening to a young man animatedly telling a story. I later learned that he was telling how he had obtained a job working under a man that he idolized. He proceeded to tell the aging professor's story, beginning with childhood and proceeding through a stellar academic career. I was inattentive but heard some of his monologue. I caught something about school and heard a sense of excitement growing as the description continued. When the young storyteller excitedly paused and sighed, I involuntarily muttered, "And then he killed her." Luckily, no one heard me. They may have thought me mad, or the purveyor of a rather unfunny joke.

This event worried me; perhaps murder as a topic of conversation or thought was becoming too commonplace for me. It was as if murder had become normal. I often struggled with this recurring worry. I had developed the sense that there was a parade of murderers that burst forth from the streets to the evening news. Almost invariably, the suspects were soon caught and placed in jail. A significant number required psychiatric evaluations. Perhaps repetition cannot help but become usual.

Those who write about film and fiction speak about the "suspension of disbelief," the viewer or reader's acceptance of a story as if it were real, forgiving inconsistencies and unlikely occurrences to allow the story to work. It is a powerful phenomenon that allows the daily viewers of television drama shows to worry over a character played by an actor who appeared on a competitor's program the year before. There is an analogous, essentially opposite reaction in work with violent persons, a suppression of emotional reaction to the horror of violence, a denial or suppression of reality to the extent that one still knows that the acts are real but does not react fully. This phenomenon is aided by the fact that the newspapers and news programs, the source of most people's information about criminals, rarely give accurate descriptions. Thus, the real murderer doesn't appear nearly as dastardly as the description that the media provides. Furthermore, if one had a violent reaction to every murderer, one could not work frequently with them. Therefore, to protect the sanctity of the mind, one becomes a bit detached and numb, as if this real murderer were fictional and the exercise in evaluating or treating him or her were practice. Fear is perhaps the emotion most carefully isolated by this process, though, at times, it comes seeping or flooding back into awareness. Although I have never consciously wished to murder anyone, including a murderer, I doubt that the feeling has been mutual.

Clark was eighteen when he first killed. The child of a poor, hardworking family, he was the first in his clan to attend college. Four months into school, he became sweepingly but silently paranoid. Perhaps part of the problem was that it was his first time away from home for any extended period. His college town was across the state from home, and it was a much bigger town than his rural village. He was well known and liked in his home town, whereas at school he was just another freshman. He began to think that the school meant him harm; he interpreted benign events with great gravity. When the school notified him of a minor rescheduling of a class, he became convinced that it was intended to "trip him up." Similarly, Clark was sure that an earnest young professor's insistence on meeting with each of his students was intended to "gather indicting information."

As part of a well-intentioned effort to decrease the sense of social and academic isolation in the freshman year, the school instituted a new program in which each freshman was assigned to work with another new student as a study partner. Unlike most of the students, Clark's study partner closely followed the rules of the program, and meekly but repeatedly insisted on the prescribed weekly meetings. Each of the students was expected to offer suggestions to his or her study partner on how to improve. Clark thought that his partner's suggestions were part of the plot. Unfortunately, Clark's study partner had a habit of referring to academic failure as "dying," as in "If you don't study all the way through the semester, you'll die on the final examination." Clark thought that the young man was threatening him. After three months of excruciating fear, Clark stabbed him to death. Not surprisingly, the study partner program died a quieter death in response. Although Clark had been paranoid for some time, he did not receive any psychiatric treatment until after the murder. This lack of a documented history

probably contributed to the fact that Clark was convicted of the murder rather than sent to a hospital as
not guilty by reason of insanity. He was sentenced to
life in prison. As a murderer, he was initially housed in
the most secure prison in the state. Full of rapists and
murderers, it was not a kind placement for a young,
psychotic college boy. Clark was soon ostracized as
a "space shot," the prison term for someone crazy.
Through this label, he was brought to the attention of
a young, naive counselor named Ernie. In professional
training in mental health, we learn that it can be
harmful to be too giving to patients. In many cases,
this harm is because giving too much fosters dependency; it does not allow the patient to begin taking responsibility for him- or herself. However, in paranoid
patients, giving can be far more dangerous, since even
the most kindhearted attention is often perceived as a
threat by such a patient. Blind to these concerns, Ernie
had his own kind but simplistic theory. He thought
that men and women were in prison due to a lack of
parental and social attention. While there is probably
some truth to his thought, his solution was to spend as
much time as he could with patients, with the most
time reserved for those patients that Ernie perceived
as the most troubled. With his look of fear and worry,
Clark was at the top of Ernie's list. Each day, Ernie
would try to spend as much time as he could with
Clark. Clark was furious and felt threatened. He was
sure that Ernie meant him harm; after all, Ernie wrote
notes in a prison chart and reviewed his case with the
correctional officers. Clark wanted to tell Ernie to go
away, but he was young and afraid that such a refusal
would bring reprisals. Clark's fear, anger, and paranoia
grew day by day. When Ernie came to his cell one day
and spent many hours there, Clark finally had enough.
He strangled Ernie with a sheet. Afterwards, Clark's
paranoia worsened as new charges were filed and he

was placed in solitary confinement. Two weeks later, a social worker came to visit him there, as the murder had brought more attention to his paranoid illness. Although she was aware of his history, Clark was able to overpower her. When the officers arrived, she was already dead. Clark was sent to the psychiatric hospital.

I had briefly met Clark at the hospital once, well before I became more substantially acquainted with him. At that point, he mentioned his name quickly, under his breath. I was not charged with his care or evaluation, so I did not ask him to repeat it. I did not connect him with his well-known reputation. He was short and slightly built. He carried himself with a certain lightness combined with purpose, like a gymnast whose every motion seemed considered and reasoned. He had a job cleaning the windows. Unlike most of the patients, he took his job very seriously. He scanned each pane, then carefully cleaned it. He made the menial job seem technical and precise. His manner led me to consider the possibility that he must doing something other than cleaning, perhaps checking the security or thermal efficiency of the windows, and that he was an employee. Only his hospital garb and the liquid window cleaner bottle gave him away.

Those who told his story spoke it with a certain deference. This respect was borne of their fear, a call back to the days when the fiercest fighter ruled. Interestingly, those who were unaware of his full clinical history ascribed to him the characteristic of fearlessness. Though he was full of fear, he did not easily show it. The expression that I grew to know as being pained appeared to be anger or even concentration to others. Indeed, one of his great problems was that Clark's fear boiled over into a rage hard to appreciate. He kept a great distance from people, and the clinical staff, mindful that his victims had been their colleagues, left him alone. One or two brave doctors exchanged a few words per week. He talked more openly to one or two others.

He had a special status at the hospital, perhaps partially due to his long stay. But the real reason was the murders. Everyone watched out for him, fussing about how to keep things steady, nonthreatening, cool, and at a distance. Although the years of therapy helped, he was still afraid of every new clinician and any change in routine or rule that affected him. He helped me see the extraordinary power of human contact. Many normal people will move thousands of miles for a romantic relationship, or even to be near relatives or a friend. They will change jobs or apartment buildings to add a touch of human contact. Clark killed repetitively to avoid it.

Clark also taught me about my own fear. I could feel the strange deference that fear creates. It was the same feeling I had as a child visiting a zoo, seeing a tiger caged and angry just a few inches and some thin poles of iron away. Of course, fear promotes a certain anger, especially in those with pride, and I felt angry that Clark received special treatment. Yet he had proved that he could kill in the time it took for an officer to come running. It took transcending my own fear to appreciate the depths of Clark's. There were those who thought that Clark was too clever for everyone, that he had wanted to be in a hospital all along, to feel special and protected. They thought that he was a cold-blooded killer masquerading as a paranoid man.

I saw Clark differently. His coldness, I thought, was due to his fear. If you are warm, people approach. He had an overwhelming fear of others and used every means to maintain distance. The strangest part of Clark was the absence of hatred in his core. I never felt hated by him, though I was sure that he would and could kill me if he felt threatened. At one time, I thought that there must be hatred for murder to occur;

in Clark's case, I believed it was all desperate fear, at a depth hard to imagine.

I thought of Clark again later, at a difficult time in my professional life. Just as I began to feel some success in my career, colleagues that I had thought would be thrilled seemed angry and envious. Sometimes, they obstructed my progress. Frustration turned into a concern about my job and the quality of support that we give each other. At some point, a fantasy of escape appeared. I would buy a cabin on a remote mountain's ridge. I'd drive into town once a week or so, at the least busy time, and buy supplies. Otherwise, I'd be alone, writing, thinking, and praying. I did not buy that cabin, but at a time when human relationships felt fragile, false, and disappointing, I understood Clark a little better.

I have been asked how many people like Clark are hidden out in the world, or in prisons. The answer is elusive; paranoid patients fear contact, which makes it hard to count them. I have seen others who were just slightly healthier than Clark. Alonzo never killed, probably due to the earlier intervention of help, yet his thoughts were more primitive than Clark's, centering on messages received in a language that did not exist for anyone else. When the messages indicated a threat, as they often did, Alonzo was swiftly brutal. Only close attention and nearly lifelong hospitalization had prevented dire consequences. Only one social worker ever understood Alonzo. While it was hard for the social worker to explain, he started with the assumption that Alonzo was honest. He believed that every utterance that Alonzo emitted was significant. He patiently asked Alonzo questions, trying to translate what many dismissed as psychotic gibberish into language. In the past, psychoanalysts attempted to do much the same thing with schizophrenic patients like Alonzo. Their work was swept out with the fever accompanying the widespread success of medications in treating psychosis. Indeed, these medications have supplanted such treatment as the mainstay. Yet, what about the patient like Alonzo, who has never significantly responded to any medication? While one patient never makes a valid research study, the only improvement I saw with him was the result of his fragile alliance with the man who served as his interpreter for the rest of humankind. Unfortunately, the social worker moved to another state, partially due to the failure of the current establishment to realize his skills.

Perhaps every field of endeavor has this problem, but the tendency of the schools of mental health to supplant the insights of one theory with a sweeping new truth is frightening. It is obvious that it is terribly hard to research psychotherapy, since the quality of the therapist and the rapport with the patient are impossibly hard to measure, and measurement might disrupt the therapy itself. When you then realize that patients often feel worse as they shift defenses (thus improving), then therapy becomes a researcher's nightmare. Yet this problem frequently results in the conclusion that therapy is not effective. It seems to be very powerful but hard to study. Alonzo's therapist had intuitively established an effective form of psychotherapy that did not fit the theoretical bias of the age. What might have been recognized as brilliant twenty years before was criticized and, worse, ignored. Although Alonzo has been kept from murder, I fear that he may decline into violence again, alone and misunderstood.

Unlike Clark or Alonzo, Mickey's all-American good looks belied his episodic paranoia. Running across the prison yard in a football game, he looked like an average young man. Indeed, despite a shy quietness, he often seemed relatively normal. His paranoia came in slow, deep waves, first a touch of suspiciousness that often silently deepened into a fearful rage. All the while, his appearance remained normal, save for the loss of his smile. Understandably, even those clinicians directly responsible for his care would sometimes fall behind in his status and not recognize the paranoia early on. He was in prison for attempted murder, having beat a stranger to a point where he was not recognized by his wife. Miraculously, the victim, who had never before met Mickey, recovered. Mickey never provided any explanation for this behavior. I never treated him, meaning that to those cold eyes and deadly arms, I was a stranger, too. He liked sports and was good at them. He appeared a bit distant, but otherwise seemed like he was engrossed in the game. But I knew his history, knew what he was capable of, and knew that becoming the focus of his paranoia was hard to predict. When I saw him playing football in the middle of the field, I took the long way around to avoid him, no matter what the weather.

17

The Poetry of
Insanity

Max was the son of a professor in a small college. His father considered himself to be a free spirit. He dabbled in various forms of politics, and more important for the future of his son, religion. Most likely, Max's father was manic–depressive. During a period of mania, he "invented" a religion that contained what he considered to be the best parts of the various religions that he had studied. Both Max and his sister were taught this religion. However, as she matured, his sister abandoned it for more traditional beliefs.

Max clung to the religion. Like his father, he was manic–depressive. However, he had more difficulties with reality, and he added strange twists to the religion after his father's death. After a series of tumultuous and short romantic relationships, Max became depressed. He also was saddened by his failure to keep a job, a difficulty no doubt due to his tendency to prose-lytize at every opportunity. In the throes of the depression, Max began to believe that the lower part of his body was evil. This section contained his legs, which had led him in the wrong direction in his pursuit of love and fulfillment. It also contained his genitalia, which he believed led him toward the wrong women, and his anus, an organ often regarded as negative. Max retained faith in the upper half, which contained his mind, the source of the religion (Max gave little credit to his deceased father). It also contained his mouth, the organ responsible for spreading the word of his beliefs. However, as the depression deepened, a happenstance altered this unusual belief in a peculiar way. Max contracted a common and minor but nonetheless disturbing infection of one eye. As this eye ached, wept, and became reddened, Max began to believe that it had been taken over by the evil lower half of his body. He began to believe that its gaze held evil portent, whereas the other, "good" eye had his true "holy" vision. Just prior to the infection, Max had met Mary, a well-meaning but impressionable young woman, who was enthralled with his intelligence. She considered him to be a visionary. Her parents recognized him as psychotic and forbade her to see him. Perhaps their prohibition increased the attraction; Max and Mary quickly married. They lived without major incident for a few months, until Max became more ill. He began to sacrifice small animals, and even Mary's regard and devotion were shaken. She moved out.

Despite a perfect recovery from the minor infection, Max still considered one eye to be evil. He began to worry that this eye had been the one that had first seen Mary. At times, he believed that she was cursed, and that she had to be sacrificed. At other times, his love for her won out and he deeply regretted his consideration of violence. This cycle worsened over time. Desperate to save Mary from his own murderous beliefs, Max damaged his own "bad" eye, rendering it blind despite surgery. The psychiatrists who treated him at the time recorded a number of poignant thoughts. Max believed that his good eye could perceive only the holy and divine in people. However, he thought that the bad eye could perceive the earthly shortcomings of humankind. In this way, he considered himself to be the powerful but sad link between the spiritual and the fallen, natural sides of humankind.

Max improved for a while, as the hospital that had served as the site of treatment for his eye also treated his psychiatric condition. However, he subsequently stopped his medication, believing that it obfuscated his religious thought. Soon, he was psychotic again.

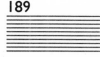
A short time later, as Mary sat alone in the park, Max came up behind her and strangled her. His psychosis never responded to treatment as it had before, I think, because his individual religion provided him with an explanation for the murder that he tried so desperately to prevent.

Max's story reveals more than the fact that he was a murderer. It demonstrates the way in which, by definition, psychosis is apart from reality but deals with real feeling. Though Max thought things that were not true, his story is full of the struggle for success, love, and integrity that we all face. Though his resolution was tragic, Max dealt with these issues in a genuine and poetic fashion. We can only wish that we were more powerful than we are and could have prevented the murder.

His story came back to me some time later, when I was struggling with the administrative policies of a hospital's bureaucracy. Despite my efforts, it felt as though the patients' interests were often forgotten. Patients often see the foibles of our systems. One of my patients had improved enough to function fairly well, and he did not understand why the schedules and constraints of the hospital often seemed to hamper his progress rather than hasten it. In an effort to ensure that I would adequately represent patients' concern at administrative meetings, I imagined that I had brought him along, knowing that his viewpoint would help me to identify changes that were not really for the benefit of him and other patients. That process continued nonetheless. I found that I enjoyed my work with the patients but not the administrative meetings. I tried to decrease my involvement with the bureaucracy, but my work was still affected by decisions that often made sense in the administration building but did not work well on the patients' units. The unit where I worked was located up the hill from the administration building. I generally walked between them. One day, I walked up toward the unit, angry about a meeting and the decisions that had just been made. I was focusing on the details at first, and I identified many unstated agendas and motives. Unlike Max, the administrators did not seem to be genuine. Although everyone couched their reasoning in terms of "what is best for the patients," the phase seemed empty, a tired slogan. I started to look at the motives and the dishonesty, and found myself becoming more angry. So I decided to try to broaden my view. I cleared my head and tried to begin at the beginning. The place was a hospital, a place for healing. People came there to feel better, to heal. Suddenly, I recognized something for the first time. The people that came for healing were not just the patients. Things were not so simple, not just as they appeared. I had learned much from my patients and had grown. The administrators and clinicians might not be aware of it, but we all have areas of our lives to work on. Suddenly, it seemed clear that a patient had more insight than some of the leaders; if allowed, he might have been able to "heal" them, or at least improve their viewpoint. Not that I felt that this fact should make the bureaucrats any less accountable. But figuratively bringing my patient to the meeting had helped my awareness and actually helped the meetings improve slightly. Over time, I saw more. I remained clear about my role as a physician, but I realized that everyone there was struggling within a crazy system and trying to find truth, clarity, and meaning. In that search, it was the patients that had helped me the most.

18

Impossible Choices

ELSA WAS almost sixty when she was sent to the state women's prison. She was gray-haired and matronly and had a kind face with hard wrinkles. She was born in a hardworking factory town to an alcoholic father and a depressed mother. Her uncle, who lived with the family when Elsa was a young teenager, was also an alcoholic. He was a smooth-talking con artist who considered himself a ladies' man. But when he got drunk and couldn't find a woman who would take him in, he raped Elsa. It took a lot of courage for Elsa to finally tell her mother, who flew into a rage and said that she would "kill that man if he ever does that," but she refused to acknowledge that it was happening. Elsa waited each night, unsure whether he would enter the room or not. The rapes didn't stop until Elsa was seventeen, and her uncle was imprisoned for forgery and assault. Prison left the family with her uncle's thirteen-year-old son. The boy's mother had abandoned him. Since Elsa's mother was depressed and her father was often drunk, most of the child-care responsibilities fell to Elsa. When she was eighteen, her father and mother died in a car crash caused by her father's drinking. Elsa continued raising her cousin Artie. Both lived in her parents' old house. Elsa worked at a factory; Artie worked more intermittently. As Artie entered his twenties, his social drinking as an adolescent had progressed into serious abuse of prescription drugs. He tried to keep his drug habit a secret from Elsa, because he knew that she would throw him out. Elsa suspected something but couldn't be harsh with Artie. She thought of Artie as her son, even though he was only four years younger.

Elsa never married, but a brief affair in her late thirties left her pregnant. The father of the child left and never helped her. Neither did Artie. Nonetheless, Elsa's daughter Kiri grew into a tall and beautiful young woman, who excelled in her studies and athletics. Pride was always evident on Elsa's face.

Elsa was fifty-two and thinking about retiring from the factory when tragedy struck. Kiri tearfully told her mother that Artie had sexually abused her three times. All of Elsa's memories of her own childhood came rushing back. She swore that she could not ignore Kiri's accusation. She called the police, the prosecutor, the school, and the local rape center. She copied down on paper what each party said to her and followed their directions dutifully. She filed charges, kicked Artie out of the house, and changed the locks. Artie was arrested, but he was released on bail because he had no previous record of any serious offenses. One afternoon, Artie tried to pick up Kiri at school. Elsa called the police and they said that they would try to keep an eye on him. A few days later, Artie grabbed Kiri on her way home from school. He raped her and beat her for getting him into trouble. Kiri didn't have to say anything when she came home. Elsa saw the bruises and the helpless desperation that she herself had felt many years before. She felt that she could not tell her daughter to wait; she could not express horror and fail to protect her daughter as her mother had done. Elsa loaded her father's old shotgun and walked with it openly visible to Artie's rooming house. She waited on the porch, and when Artie came home, she shot him dead.

A jury found her guilty of murder. The separation from Kiri hurt her the most, but she remained philosophical. She said, "I had to choose between my own

child and the man I raised as my own child, and I
couldn't have chosen any other way."

The court decided that Elsa had another choice,
that of waiting for the authorities to arrest and im-
prison Artie. Yet from Elsa's experience of years of in-
action came an understandable expectation that any
delay was too much.

The courts and attorneys operate on what I call
"legal time." Although they often are busy and rushed,
the courts sometime examine one aspect of a serious
case in exquisite (or excruciating) detail. An event of
two minutes duration may be examined for hours in
court, and for much longer, if the preparation of attorneys and experts is included. Although there may be
some statements made to avoid it, the effect is that
time is slowed. A moment's choice may thus seem open
to an exhaustive number of options and considerations.

Moreover, the proceedings are conducted in a
wood-lined, temperature-controlled environment with
discourse by relatively well paid and well educated
people. There is often a pervasive assumption that the
world outside works according to laws, too. There is a
tacit agreement that each person functions according
to the legal requirement of his or her job or relationship. As if, upon awakening, before or after brushing
his or her teeth, a person checks the relevant statutes
applicable to the activities of the day. The justice system is inexorable in the application of its rules to others, but it rarely realistically assesses itself with such
rigor. Large organizations have aped this worldview by
creating an ever more complex set of policies and procedures, whose main function seems to be to give the
courts something to look at when things go wrong.

I have conjured up an imaginary patient who has
some inherited income, allowing him or her to spend all
day poring over the laws trying to be sure he or she is
obeying each one. The laws are so many and confusing

that many are ignored and unenforced, and thus are functionally nonexistent. Some scholars believe removing all rules or laws would never lead to anarchy because some would immediately return by agreement or convention. I sometimes wonder whether we aren't instead approaching lawlessness in the other direction, by creating so many laws that, rather than moving toward zero, we are trying to approach infinity.

The fact that most, perhaps all, people function not primarily by law means that this unacknowledged court view is fiction. Having not faced what is often a hard reality, they have constructed a fictional one. In that world, Elsa was guilty. Murder may often represent a seemingly impossible choice and perhaps a truly impossible one.

Roger was only twenty-three when I met him. He was very intelligent, and equally paranoid. He showed little eye contact. There were only little glances to check if you were listening to his highly technical conversation, which he would continue for hours if not redirected. He was convinced that the police planned to kill him, but that they planned to torture him by slowly revealing small hints about the form and date of the murder for years before it happened. He interpreted a variety of minor events as constituting these clues. Two years previously, he had added together a number of clues to the fixed conclusion that he would be murdered by a young, uniformed officer on his birthday. He bought a life insurance policy, gave notice on his apartment, and prepared a detailed will. Nonetheless, he hoped to avoid his fate, and he armed himself with a gun. When a young officer walked up the block at an time that Roger thought might be the appointed hour, Roger shot him. After he was found not guilty by reason of insanity and placed in a secure hospital, he was very opposed to medications to treat his psychosis. Unlike most patients who oppose such treatment, Roger believed he would improve, but not because of the medication's effectiveness. He believed that the police would stop giving clues exactly when he started medication. Thus, when asked about symptoms after the medication started, he would say that he was not perceiving any clues. The doctor would believe that the medication was improving his delusions. Thus, Roger believed that his apparent improvement would "prove" that his allegations were "crazy." He was caught in an elaborate web of his own paranoia, such that even the choice to improve was blocked. Within the confines of his beliefs, he had no choices. On an intellectual level, he could answer any questions related to his beliefs in a way that never allowed any challenge to penetrate. Yet on rare occasions, there was genuine emotion, never associated with words. For a second, he would look at me with a genuine sadness. His situation was not what he believed it to be, but my version of it was just as tragic as his.

Roger's case always reminded me of a young schizophrenic woman who was not a murderer, but who also resisted improvement in her mental condition for a poignant reason. She heard voices that told her that she would witness the return of Jesus and would see miracles upon this return. This woman heard a voice one day telling her to climb atop an electric pole. She was electrocuted and badly injured. Despite multiple surgeries, she was unable to walk, yet she still had faith in the voices and the miracles that they would reveal. She believed that one of the miracles that she would witness would be her return to health; she resisted treatment of her psychosis because it removed her greatest hope.

19

The Child Child Murderer

THE TERM *psychotic regression* has fallen into disuse. It hearkens back to the days when American psychiatry was more psychoanalytic, and delusions and hallucinations were thought to represent, in part, a return to a pattern of dream-like thought seen in children and infants. Today, we are caught in a wave of increased biological research and theory in which psychosis is seen as an imbalance of chemical transmitters in the brain. My suspicion is that both ideas are simplistic; psychotic thought is probably neither a pathological return to infancy nor a simple running out of a particular neural "gasoline."

Yet psychotic regression does describe some patients extraordinarily well. These are men and women who seem to become quite child-like—docile but prone to tantrums, simple but coy. Ernest was a fifty-seven-year-old little boy. It is hard to imagine Ernest as a murderer. He generally walked around with a silly smile and was usually polite and playful. Many would suspect that his childish demeanor was the product of years of institutionalization, but its roots were deeper. Indeed, Ernest, when psychotic, considered himself to be a young boy. At times, he noticed his aging face and felt that it was a cruel trick.

Ten years before, Ernest was living at home with his elderly mother. One day, she had gone to the grocery store. Ernest enticed some children into the house with cookies and soda. Three children entered; they played board games and drew pictures. Only two left. Ernest stabbed one little girl for reasons that are unclear. He had said it was because he wanted to save her, though from what is uncertain. Some clinicians hypothesized that she threatened to tell his mother. It is tempting to think that part of the problem was that Ernest thought that he was the same age as the girl, and that her death resulted from his literally not knowing his own strength. Yet psychosis is not a return to normal childhood. Ernest's view of the world was profoundly depressed. It seems likely that he found little success in adulthood— his mother was highly critical, and his illness limited his abilities for external rewards. At that time, the community had few programs for mentally ill persons. Childhood may have seemed preferable, an escape from an unhappy adulthood. Maybe childhood had been better or was at least recalled as such. Ernest would oscillate between an uncomfortable and partial acceptance of adulthood and a delusional and awkward return to childhood. Perhaps he retained the knowledge that the little girl would also have to face the same challenge, that she could not save herself from the inevitability of growing up. Yet there may have been more than a sad rescue in his act. Perhaps he resented that she really was the child that he so desperately wanted to be.

Ernest's case also illustrates another aspect of psychosis. Reality is a matter of perspective. Many "normal" persons drive bumper to bumper at breakneck speeds in the traffic jams in Boston and other major cities. Although we may question the ecological wisdom of our commuting patterns, we only question the individual's sanity in jest (or if just cut off by that individual). It is an old maxim in psychiatry that psychosis looks less and less unreal as one examines it more closely. Or, as one of my teachers put it, the person seems faced with a choice between an unacceptable reality or a workable unreality. Ernest's adult life was filled with rejection and disfavor. It seems possible that he attempted to escape into childhood. Indeed, many of us occasionally share this fantasy. When Ernest escaped, he found that the hate did not disappear.

For me, Ernest also illustrated the illusory capabilities of our memory. Like the aging veterans who seem to recall wars fought long-ago with the alacrity of the latest baseball game, we remember our childhood as the picture book stories that we read. Yet many people (both patients and not) have suffered varying levels of abuse in childhood. Patients who have suffered extreme levels of abuse often have no recollection of the experiences. They seem to have sheltered their ongoing life from the direct memory, although its effects are still often felt as nightmares, flashbacks, and, sadly, a tendency for revictimization.

What about the current controversy surrounding people who recall abuse as a child and confront the suspected abuser in court years later? There seems to be two schools of thought regarding this topic. There is the view proffered by the therapists in such cases that the abuse occurred as recalled, and that the court case will be healing for the victim. The alternative view is that memory is faulty, and that memories are suggested by overzealous therapists. This latter view is supported by some research that says that suggestion can alter memory, and that it is a frail faculty. It is only mildly amusing that the proponents of this view are often experts in court themselves, presumably relying on their own weak memories.

The therapists perhaps fear that the view opposing theirs is a retreat to a time when childhood abuse was often considered to be a fantasy. Indeed, that sometimes is precisely what the other side is suggesting. Yet some cases have supported the alleged abuser, fingering the therapist as implanting false memories.

There is, I believe, a middle ground. Therapists conduct therapy. A therapeutic truth need not be an "actual one." What if the "false" memory of abuse by a father was due to actual abuse by another father figure? What if the abuse was not in the form recalled, but subtler and still powerful? My point is that I believe that the resolution lies in keeping therapeutic truths in the therapy room. Evaluations for court cases should, I believe, be separate from the therapy and the therapist. Moreover, my experience with the legal system suggests that it is rarely the site of a healing experience. That statement does not mean that people should never pursue the legal aspects; it just should be separate from the therapy.

As for the memory issue, we have known it to be faulty all along. The frailties are not limited to therapeutic suggestion, but to every coached and cross-examined witness (and expert). We have to conduct legal matters within the uncertainty of recollection.

Recollection of childhood is distorted for many people. Even those of us who struggled with our parents and suffered lesser forms of mistreatment at the ebbs of their lives seem ill-equipped to recall the downside of a childhood that seems to become increasingly filled with carnivals and ice cream as senescence nears. Ernest's recollections of his sexual abuse as a child, recalled with vivid clarity, were the likely source of his aggression. For me, they stirred the darker corners of my soul and helped me to recall the easily forgotten, colder parts of my experience as a child. In this, I felt a faint recapitulation of the murder. Ernest killed my illusion of my nearly always happy child. There is no horror worse than childhood fear and death, and it is odd that this childish, harmless-looking older man stirred a deeper horror in me than most of the evil-looking and threatening young killers. He also made it more daunting for me to consider having children, because Ernest didn't look evil. Every baby-sitter and schoolyard attendant would be suspect.

20

In the Gang

GANGS ARE again a focus of attention. For many people, they are a source of understandable fear and perhaps evidence of a society gone astray. It is hard, maybe impossible, to dispute this view. There is no logic to young men shooting everyone in a house because of some disagreement. Many times, the argument is over large sums of money generated in the drug trade. Sometimes, the violence is related to territory. Yet in many cases, it is the type of argument that would, we think, lead to only a raised voice or a wrestling bout with a few punches. This worry is one of the most pervasive in discussions of gangs; the fear is that violence can occur for a reason so minimal as to be ludicrous. In this way, the deaths seem beyond understanding and beyond history.

The difficulty that I have with this viewpoint is that feigning lack of understanding increases fear without bringing solutions. Small guns that shoot at amazing speed and accuracy are relatively new. Gangs are not new. I see less of a fundamental difference between the gangs of today and those of yesterday than most. The killings are usually for fear, love, money, power, or honor. Honor? Is it ridiculous to speak of honor when discussing gangs? Perhaps the honor is not the kind that most of us wish to promote. Yet I see the "honor" of gangs as flowing from a long tradition of violence. Leaving aside the roving gangs of Europe, the early colonists and the Western pioneers were violent territorialists. For both, law was a later development. Similarly, the gangsters of Prohibition have been romanticized in

207

fiction and film, but the blood flowed as red as today. It is easy to argue that there is something more wretched about the gangs of today. Strangely, I both agree and disagree. I see the same signs of awe for the gangs now as for those that have gone before. Legions of younger children dress the part at suburban shopping malls. We all see the films in which the overt message is to avoid the gang. The excitement comes from the gang's violence. I can see a future in which these gangs are the subject of the same ambivalent reverie of the gangsters of the days of Prohibition, an ambivalence that fades as time passes.

Yet there may be differences. Much of the rancor today may be barely concealed racism. Maybe, too, the causes are different. I don't really know what the families and neighborhoods of the old gangsters were like. For some wretched individuals today, murder seems so much a predictable outcome of violent lives that it could be considered no less than natural for that person. I met Ike when he was seventeen. His mother was too young to have remembered Dwight Eisenhower, the president whose nickname she chose for her son's name. Perhaps she named him after the musical performer Ike Turner. His gang friends changed it to Ice, the street name of the version of amphetamine that could be smoked. It was an apt nickname; Ike had all the characteristics of a person under the effects of that drug, even when he wasn't able to use it. He was fast-talking, witty, violent, and deeply paranoid. He hid the latter characteristic beneath a layer of stylized talk designed to impress his fellow gang members and anyone else in earshot. He would often say, "He doesn't do nothing for me," seeming to mean that he was not impressed with a particular character. Yet these were almost code words for Ike. They secretly meant that the man hadn't reassured Ike that his deeply suspicious assumptions were not true.

Ike was born into a difficult situation. He was a thin, white boy in a predominantly African-American neighborhood. He was regularly beaten by his drunk mother, her string of ne'er-do-well boyfriends, and the neighborhood toughs. Over time, he built up an endless well of violent anger. Combined with the drugs and possibly a genetic predisposition for schizophrenia, he became paranoid. He thought that he could hear the neighborhood talking about him from his room. Furthermore, he thought that he could read all of the thoughts of persons from the expression on their faces. Indeed, he had a razor-sharp insight and did see much in the movements and glances of others. Using these skills, Ike transcended the usual racial barriers of urban life and became a key member of a predominantly African-American gang. He had probably participated in a number of murders, but he was arrested for a brutal assault on a young woman that, if not interrupted, may have ended in rape and murder. Ike and others taught me much about the gang leaders. These were not men or women who loved or enjoyed death. They simply did not value their own lives or others enough to consider death a serious step. No sudden change need occur for the murder to happen, save for the appearance of a place and victim. The term *unfolding* often came to mind for me with my work with these usually young men, for whom the murder came as easily as the next page in this book. Those of us who value life often want to ascribe some more meaningful explanation for this behavior. Some want to claim that the failure to value life is a form of depression or psychosis. In Ike's case, he was in fact psychotic. His paranoia reached beyond even the immense amount of suspicion that one would consider normal for the life of a violent youth. He heard voices. In prison, he developed a deeply held set of beliefs in which all of the activities of the prison were directed around him. He was sure that everyone, including other prisoners, were watching him in order to report to the warden and his gang leader.

Yet, most gang leaders probably are not psychotic, at least not in a clinical sense. Even their loss of a sense of the value of life is unfortunately not terribly unrealistic in the setting of their upbringing and neighborhood. Most may not even be depressed, although for many, their viewpoint is a sad one. They only strive for a short, fast life in which all impulses are fulfilled, including the one for death.

Gang members who are not the leaders or instigators of violence may join in because of peer pressure, fear of injury by an opposing gang, or fear of shame or reprisal of their own gang members who are watching. They may have other limited opportunities for a sense of belonging, as well as protection. But even my distinction between leaders and followers is too easy. Sometimes, the leader is scared, too, but there may be no one in a position to question the violence, especially when the other gangs seem unlikely to pursue peace.

Research indicates that the life expectancy for a child in a poor, violent section of a city in the United States is quite low. Non–gang members get caught in the crossfire or killed by having some association with a gang member. Although the brave souls that choose not to join may have a better chance statistically, it may appear that they are accepting death in a purely passive manner rather than defending themselves. I see a striking parallel in the opening scenes of American Civil War movies in which the sons are implored to protect some sacred ideal supposedly represented by the Army. In the gangs, membership may feel more inevitable because it is a war that never ends.

I am not excusing or condoning gang violence. I am saying that to understand it, we have to look at it squarely. Doing so is frightening, because we see an organized chaos that makes a dangerous mockery of our ideas of history, civilization, and society.

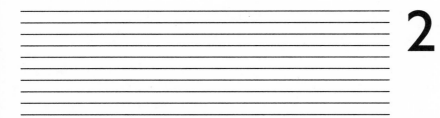

21

Baby Death

I RECENTLY returned from a trip to New York City. The cab drivers caught my fascination. Despite varying nationalities and dispositions of character, each of the drivers displayed a remarkably similar style of driving. In searching for the words to describe it, my mind alit on one of those purposefully ambiguous phrases so favored by modern advertisers. The driving style was "pedestrian peril." Clearly, one meaning of the phrase indicates the danger to those who walked in front of the cabs. They were in peril indeed, as each cabby accelerated in any open section of street, squeezed through any hole, and subverted the clause that traffic may proceed after pedestrians have cleared. I do not know the rates of pedestrian death by cab, but I was amazed at the skill of the city residents in establishing a rhythm and a keen eye for the charging yellow cab. Nonetheless, agility must fail at times.

I experienced a silent shudder on one of the last taxi rides of my visit. Perhaps the driver was imperceptibly more dangerous, or my denial was wearing thin. I began to imagine a scene. A cab takes a passenger to one of the sad, decrepit, and rotting corners of the city. Perhaps it is night. In the midst of a populous city, this section feels remote. Few other cars appear. Many of the streetlamps are broken; the remaining lights flicker. Of course, after discharging his rider, the cab has no one to take back to the center of town. For the sake of getting back to earning, and perhaps because of fear, he drives even faster than usual. He covertly imagines that the neighborhood is as desolate

213

as it appears, a true "no man's land." He careens around corners faster than usual and runs red lights when no one is visible. As his pace quickens further, he nears the edge of the neighborhood. Suddenly, he sees a flash. He questions his imagination until he hears the thud and sees that he has hit a child.

My mind races at this point in the daydream. I pray that he stops, or at the least, uses the radio to call. In fact, my daydream continues with only the nauseating kindness (if it can even be so termed) of backing up a few feet to avoid a second hit. The driver thus avails himself of a momentary assessment before he screeches off. I would hope that the driver would feel some sorrow, or at least fear. I could not help but wonder if any such deaths occur in the bowels of that city. My fear is that the driver would just keep going, letting the memory fade with the endless blocks of the city and the clicks of the meter.

This fear is rooted in the ease with which laws and lines of car and pedestrian travel were broken. Time after time, the cars squeezed through bare gaps, between a truck and an elderly woman, between a high curb and a school bus. They always seemed to err on the curbside, resulting in an accumulation of scars, painted over in slight variations of the original yellow.

The coolness of the drivers in these perilous maneuvers bothered me most. As they endangered numerous citizens, themselves, and me, they were calm. Indeed, each driver found some other absorbing activity to divert his attention. One unsuccessfully tried to fix his car telephone. Another paged through a book of maps, never slowing his car as he pursued a yet uncertain destination. This casualness in the face of danger is the other meaning of "pedestrian peril." As my time in cabs accumulated during this trip, my anger grew at this distracted aloofness to reckless behavior. It also reminded me of my own ability to become accustomed to murder and murderers.

Every so often, when murder had become common-place for me, one murder would break the pattern. Like no other, the news of a baby killing would send a shudder down my spine. I am not alone in this horror. Society has the least forgiveness for infanticide; even prisoners will kill a baby murderer for the crime itself.

Katrina was a young woman who had moved to the United States from Europe. She had little money when she made the trip, but she persevered. She first found work as a maid and saved her money. After becoming a U.S. citizen, she qualified for a scholarship. While still cleaning houses part-time, she attended college. After graduation, she worked as a receptionist for a lawyer, then for a real estate agency. When a sales person unexpectedly quit, Katrina was trained and promoted. She was a natural saleswoman, bright, polished, and persuasive. Within two years, she was the top performing sales associate at the agency. Money began pouring in. She bought a large house and a fancy car. Through her previous employer, she met a young lawyer, and a year later, they married. Through her new husband, Katrina became introduced to the social functions of the successful young people in the city. She was a hit at the parties and found that her new acquaintances often became customers, furthering her financial success. At the parties, Katrina also developed a taste for cocaine. Her husband initially disapproved but eventually joined her in the habit. Although they minimized the importance of their addiction, they were hooked. It rapidly became an expensive habit, but the couple's prodigious income allowed them to avoid resorting to crime to keep using the drug.

Katrina was able to keep up appearances at the job, but she and her husband lost their discipline in other ways. They both became gaunt and tired looking. They were inconsistent in their use of birth control, and Katrina became pregnant. She had hoped to wait a few years, but she wanted to have the baby. She knew that cocaine would harm the fetus, so Katrina spent the entire nine months of gestation in the remote European village where she had been raised. She craved cocaine but was able to avoid it away from the life she had constructed in the United States.

Upon the birth of her baby, Katrina returned to the United States. She hired a nanny, returned to work, and soon thereafter, to cocaine. The negative effects of the drug began to accumulate. Katrina was always tired when she wasn't high, and she was often irritable. During her absence, her husband had indulged in an affair. When Katrina learned about it, she kicked him out of the house. Her cocaine use soon increased. One evening, the baby's nanny could not stay because of an illness in her family. Katrina could not find a baby-sitter on short notice, so she stayed home with the baby. She tried to avoid using cocaine that night, but this avoidance of her frequent use led to headaches and severe craving. She searched the house but was out of the drug. Her usual supplier could not bring any to her, as he had been arrested. In desperation. Katrina bundled the baby into the car and set out in search of cocaine. She soon found an old source and came home with a large supply. However, the trip had disrupted the baby's usual pattern of sleep and food. The infant was fussy and irritable. Katrina's use of the drug didn't help her own irritability. She tried food, milk, sleep, walking, and driving, but the baby wouldn't stop crying. Katrina's annoyance grew, and her increased dose of cocaine didn't help. Finally, she lashed out and slapped the baby. She hadn't meant to hit hard, but she thrust the baby's head against the crib with such force that the infant was dead on arrival at the hospital.

Katrina was sent to a secure psychiatric unit for evaluation, as her defense lawyer was considering an insanity plea. Katrina readily admitted that she had

no history of mental illness, and that she was not psychotic at the time of the death. Still, she blamed the
baby's death on the drug. She acted as if the cocaine
were a deadly ghost that had crept inside of her, raised
her hand, and sent it hurling down. She kept saying, "I
would never do a thing like this." Many murderers of
passion react in this way. They cannot accept the idea
of themselves as the agents of their deadly actions.
They search for some reason, some external agent to
explain it. They are often aided by their attorneys, who
need to provide a defense. I suspect that this scenario
explains the recent use of various medications and
even snack foods as defenses against murder charges.
The difficulty is that this form of denial delays their
eventual acceptance of their responsibility for their
action.

At some level, Katrina appreciated the gravity of
her action. If she had any difficulty, the other inmates
reminded her with their jeers and horrid imitations of
baby cries. Even a woman who killed her fifteen-year-
old sister called Katrina a profane name. Despite
Katrina's partial understanding, she used the drug
problem as the sole explanation of her actions. She became obsessed with substance-abuse treatment. Within a month, she was spouting all of the catchwords of
Narcotics Anonymous and every paperback that she
could find in the library. Her incessant, unthinking,
and, ultimately, unfeeling answer to any inquiry was
"It was the drugs."

I tried to understand why I, like the prisoners,
seemed to be less forgiving of Katrina than other
killers. A friend reminded me of an event that had occurred when I was in high school. A group of us had
gone to see a movie without knowing too much about it
beforehand. The movie was powerful and tense. It involved a young, angry, and troubled father. There was
a set of scenes in which he was alone with his infant

son or daughter. The baby began to cry and the father's face moved from disaffection to disappointment to anger. He got up, moved away, and appeared to be heading, inexorably, to hurt his child. These cinematic events took a few minutes, but they seemed like hours. I surprised all of my friends by getting up and leaving the theater before this scene came to an end.

Not all of my work has involved murderers. I have cared for other patients, some with severe illness who are relatively helpless. When the system fails these voiceless people, when an administrator makes a decision that adversely affects them, my anger flares. While this self-revelation may sound virtuous, there are times when I have taken on too much in my attempt to speak for the silent, and have raised my voice to deaf ears.

Intellectually, I can see Katrina's plight. I know that no mother or father has not contemplated infanticide. I know that it was her choice to take cocaine, but once taken, her judgment was not the same. On the emotional side, however, the empathy I can raise for Katrina is slight. I keep thinking of the baby.

I cannot forgive Katrina, although I appreciate that she will have to endure endless emotional pain. The mourning of one's own victim may be the worst grief of all. All grief involves some fantasy of blame or control. We wonder if we could have said or done something differently. When the blame is real, the mourning may be endless.

For a mother or father, killing an infant is killing a recent issue from inside. It is perhaps the closest murder to suicide. Societally, it is the least forgivable murder. For many ancient peoples, the sacrifice of a child was a solemn and holy ritual, the ultimate sacrifice. Today, it may be a declaration of ultimate self-absorption. Katrina could not keep herself from cocaine for one night. She had a nanny every other night. Because

of her success, everyone at work doted on Katrina.
That night, her baby needed her but couldn't ask in an
ingratiating and satisfying way. Katrina needed constant satisfaction and doomed herself to endless pain. 21 Baby Death

22

The Doctor Voyeur and the Murderer Inside

WORKING WITH murderers forced me to reexamine my own childhood. As a defense, each of us glosses over the pains of our younger years as we age, slowly replacing the truth with the euphemistic versions we tell strangers, until our recall matches these scrubbed and polished rewrites. Specifically, I began to recall my own relationship with violence. I am also quite sure that this recollection was related to my relentless search for my reasons for choosing this career.

In elementary school, I was the second-shortest kid in the class. To make matters worse, I was skinny and looked younger than my age (two attributes that, thankfully, later changed to assets). The other boys picked on me. Each time this occurred, I followed a certain pattern. At first, I ignored it and avoided the other boy. Then, if the ridicule continued over time, I reached my threshold. At that point, the other boy became "fair game." The first few fights in my young career were clear losses. I ended up angrier and more ridiculed. But, after maybe seven fights, I began to catch on to fighting. Although I didn't take any lessons, I picked up pointers from boxing and karate movies. I also took a picture book on martial arts out of the library. I was far from a master, but I learned to be brave, strike quickly, and protect myself. Although I never included these feelings in my euphemistic version, by the tenth or eleventh fight, I enjoyed myself. I hit hard and fast, and began to win. Soon, I eagerly awaited a new foe. Indeed, if the ridicule began, I provoked the other boy, egging him on to reach the threshold. Somehow, I never

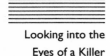
got into it with the really big kids. By the end of elementary school, my fighting days were mostly over. The punishments for fighting in school began to loom larger, and I began to slowly catch up in size.

Only Larry Howell and I still fought. He and I were two of the few boys our age in the neighborhood, so we were always either fighting or friends. We were about the same size, both sometimes arrogant, often bored, and evenly matched. I cannot recall any of the specific reasons for the fights. I think that we both enjoyed them, and when we ran out of friendly things to do, one or the other would get to pushing or insulting.

This pattern subsided when my family moved to another neighborhood in the same school district. I continued growing, but Larry really grew. By the beginning of high school, he was starting on the varsity football team. Unfortunately, he was placed directly behind me in the assigned seats of a class. I guess he was bored, because he began taunting me and throwing pieces of paper down my shirt. I glared back at him, reckoning that his height and arm length must have given him about a foot's better reach. I also knew that fighting in high school could mean expulsion. I was annoyed, but I tried to raise my threshold. He kept at it, however, and that forty- or fifty-minute class seemed to drag on for days. Finally, I'd had enough and the old feelings came back. I whipped around and quickly shoved his desk into his chest. As I turned back around, his calculator slid to the tile floor with a deadening clunk. He tried to click it on, but it was broken. At this point, the other boys in the class began to murmur about a fight. One young man, smaller than I, happily informed me that Larry had a significantly longer reach. I was at least a bit scared but prepared for the fight. No set time was made, but I was told to be "ready" that afternoon. The tension rose as nothing happened through the afternoon school periods. I began to notice a sense of some disappointment mixed with relief as the last period ended and I walked to the door. Suddenly, I felt a rush of air behind me. As I began to turn, my books were pushed out of my arm. I instinctively followed them down, and as I finished gathering them, Larry had swiftly disappeared. Unbruised (and amused), I thus ended my fighting career. However, in the later years of high school, one of my friends frequently involved us in a series of face-offs with another group in which insults were hurled and fighting was threatened. These episodes never progressed, partially because my friend, who was so vehement in his insults from a distance, became more agreeable as the other group approached.

These memories came back to me in my work with violent criminals because, in my euphemistic retelling of these stories, I have omitted the fact that I was addicted to violence. I like to think that I outgrew this predilection, but the least astute Freudian thinker may guess that the sense of affirmation that I achieved in the schoolyard, my career, and this volume are related. The frightening part of this realization came to me when I was working with violent patients on a nearly daily basis. Quite simply, I worried about my underlying wishes. My stated goal was a reduction of violence, but what did that elementary student inside of me want?

Concerned about these thoughts, I searched for any ways in which I was actually promoting violence rather than reducing it. Thankfully, I found nothing horrific. I did notice that I was fond of a number of patients who, within the hospital or prison, had taken on a role similar to my own in school. They had a history of previous assaults that kept them safe. They had not repeated their violence since I worked with them. Relieved to find no direct way in which I was unconsciously undoing my stated objective, I began to trace a more subtle, less dangerous, but no less disturbing behavior pattern in myself and my colleagues.

In a classical psychiatric paradigm that attempted to explain young men with antisocial behavior, the son's exploits are covertly rewarded by the father, who secretly enjoys them. Using this idea, we can imagine two similar fathers. One lives vicariously but doesn't reward his son for misbehavior; instead, he doesn't adequately discipline him. Alternatively, the other father viciously punishes his son to overcompensate for his secret affirmation of the behavior. I have seen each of these scenarios and, less commonly, analogous versions with mothers and daughters. No one should feign surprise at this phenomenon, since our society's taste for the angry hero appears to be hardly met by the endless spring of films extolling the glory of youthful rage.

But before I protest too much, what about my motives for entering the secret world of the murderer? As a psychiatrist, I was allowed access to the minds of the most dangerous members of society. It was a violence voyeur's dream, and as I realized the roots of my own fascination with violence, my own voyeurism became clear. I could not detect, and hope I am immune from, enjoyment of assaults, but I was fascinated with the stories, the plots, and the determinants of violence. My interest was not purely academic. As I explored my childhood, I realized that I was again proving my bravery. Thinking back on previous discourses with colleagues and staff, it became clear that some of my more passionate intonations about the prevention of violence were attempts at compensating for my voyeurism. Completing the paradox, I also was heartened to find a compensatory distaste for violence. Some psychiatrists think that all of our most seemingly altruistic efforts in life are vain compromises with our evil impulses. Having spent no small effort at treating and understanding violence, it is sobering to wonder if my interest had its roots in morbid curiosity.

While hardly cleansed of my own voyeurism, I soon began to detect similar behavior in colleagues. At a meeting, one professional gave an impassioned monologue on the violence in pornography. Of course, he provided slides of lewd and lurid examples of the wrongful craft. With each slide, his condemnation rose an octave. One of the slides depicted an advertisement for a particularly objectionable low-budget publication. Although it seemed to me that the advertisement itself was explicit and explicative enough, the speaker added that he'd had to send in two orders to receive his copy. Despite his dire warnings of the potential outcomes of the proliferation of such publications, it was quite obvious to me that his interest was more than academic.

Perhaps this difficulty is no worse than in the rest of medicine. We certainly want doctors to be fascinated by their work, yet their sworn pledge is to fight the very disorders that so interest them. But voyeurism for murder and rape is far more sinister than that for pneumonia. I admit to having developed no stunning resolution of this issue, although I am carefully aware of my own behavior when my own curiosity is aroused.

On a Friday afternoon during a period of intense work with violent patients, a colleague asked me how I was doing. He asked with a smile; both of us had experienced a grueling month or two. Each day was filled with stressful decisions, interviews, meetings with patients, and reports to be dictated and corrected. Yet that Friday brought a brief respite. We had both caught up with our work. Since neither of us had required duties in the late afternoon, he suggested that we leave early and see a movie. Though we had worked hard, it felt like a truant escape. As we drove away, he reviewed the options at the local theaters. I had lost track of the latest offerings. He strongly encouraged a futuristic adventure film in which humans and androids battle each other in a nearly incessant rattle of gunfire. I thought that I had lost interest in such films years before, although I had not tested this hypothesis by seeing one. He prevailed, and I thoroughly enjoyed the movie. It still strikes me as embarrassing, because I am concerned about the potentially damaging effects of media violence. Yet, on that day, it was truly cathartic.

In thinking back on the weeks before I saw the film, I remember grappling with the issue of repeat offenders. After spending time in prison, many inmates come back again, sometimes having committed a worse crime on the second round. For anyone who worked with the inmate during the previous sentence, the second crime feels like a failure. Indeed, it is, although it may be foolish to think that any psychiatrist can take away the many causes of violence from anyone else. But that week, my heart was heavy. I saw the worry of a senior psychiatrist who had nurtured vast improvement in a mentally ill prisoner prior to his release, only to see the man back again on charges of aggravated assault. The doctor had not released the man, but the story weighed heavily upon both of us. The movie was this inmate's story turned inside out. In the film, the main character had an undeservedly bad reputation. By confronting a series of nightmarishly horrible, partially alive, electronic gizmo-monsters, he proved something (I am still not sure what). On the one hand, the movie, in fantasy, changed the outcome of my older colleague's dilemma. The movie character was repetitively violent, but we were inescapably led to believe that he had no choice. Sadly, of course, the real inmate's violence was not inescapable and apparently deliberate.

Of course, the film also strongly echoed my investigation of the effects of voyeurism. It was an utterly engrossing film, fast-paced, and quite literally electric.

I could allow my voyeurism full rein because the story was fictional. It was, as many say, "just a movie." Yet, in the days that followed, I again worried about the larger effects of these films. For many people, such a film might be seen as a confirmation of a violent approach to the world rather than a catharsis. I cannot convincingly argue for the elimination of such films, and yet I cannot support them either.

As this intellectual debate continued in my mind, a more personal sense emerged. As the film played, I had become the main character fighting my way out. Most films are effective in promoting this identification of the audience with the protagonist. One recent sequel even convincingly made the evil character from the first film the protagonist in the second. As I pondered the thought of all of the varied members of the audience becoming the murderous hero of the film, I recalled a poetic riddle that I wrestled with in childhood. After reading a series of somber novels about the human condition, I decided that perhaps everyone commits a murder. I did not mean that each person actually shoots or stabs someone, but that those who do not directly murder kill through avarice, ignorance, or unkindness. A wealthy executive may fire two hundred people from the sanctity of his office; later, one or more may die indirectly. A well-stuffed urbanite may eat some gourmet delight on a high floor of a secure building as someone dies of starvation some yards under her unseeing glance. Even less directly, youthful souls in a zestful quest for progress may kill the spirit of traditions that have gone before, unknowingly killing the life spirit of the aged, who dare not live past the life span of the culture that sustained them. Needless to say, I was not always a carefree youth.

These thoughts came back as I contemplated my work with "real" murderers. For me, the most personally compelling sense derived from contact with murderers was neither horror nor shock. Those feelings faded with time and with greater exposure to murderers, even those whose crimes and lives filled the news shows and columns. For one thing, prison is a great equalizer; everyone is in drab clothes and surroundings. Furthermore, news articles and descriptions emphasize the exciting parts. For the duration of a moment of television time or a column of newspaper, the murderer is a "cunning monster." The news people don't see them long enough to note that many are slightly built, and that most are nervous. Murder is no less a crime, but it is amazing how similar these people are to the rest of us. Strains of the cold killer are present in all of us when stress shuts down our compassion. Indeed, everyone fantasizes about murder and it is not accidental that the overwhelmingly popular films and books place the protagonist in a situation in which violence appears to be the only way out. Perhaps our shock and horror about murder, and the media's hyperbole, are not only a result of its devastation and senselessness. Maybe it is more than selling papers. Behind the steep walls and barbed fences, safe from deeper scrutiny, the actual murderer remains unrecognizable. The media's harsh descriptions make us seem very different from them; we feel virtuous within the appearance of this vast distance between ourselves and the murderer. Those murderers found to have lived unnoticed in the midst of suburbia are later described as all the more cunning. Inevitably, someone comes forward with a description of heretofore unknown eccentricities that could have served as clues and identify the murderer as aberrant, figuratively outside the ranks of his or her neighbors. Yet perhaps these efforts represent our striving to remove from sight our own darker side.

Seeing that movie with my friend helped me to begin an exploration of my own darker side. Some time after I saw it, I started to notice a daydream. It involved an escape from a prison or secure hospital. Sometimes, it was just a glimpse, like a preview for a movie—night, the sound of helicopters, spotlights veering wildly, catching the glint of the razor wire fences. At other times, I would plan it out a bit more, or let the scene run.

I remember part of one daydream clearly. The view is from above, from a helicopter hovering over a grassy field between the buildings. There is a flurry of activity on the periphery—more helicopters, guards trying to repel the invaders or running for cover, inmates looking for a hole in the fence. The helicopter is coming down to the place that was agreed upon, to pick up the person that is the object of the mission. The grass is long, longer than they ever let it grow. It begins to flatten and then turns wildly as the helicopter approaches. Suddenly, I can see that the inmate being rescued is me.

Some time before the daydream, I had written an academic article about the possibility that some people worked in correctional jobs because they had an unconscious desire for punishment. When I wrote the article, I included myself in my consideration. I was aware that I demanded a lot of myself, and that there were childhood issues that I avoided, even in my own psychotherapy.

It was not until years later that I revisited this time and realized that I was carrying a larger dark desire for penance. It was made up of a lot of things, including guilt about my love for those elementary school fights and the blame that children may feel for their parents' divorce. It took me a while to realize that the academic paper, although still accurate for others, was also about me at a deeper level. In a symbolic way, my ruminations and theories about violence were about me too. In a different daydream, I saw myself rambling around dark corridors of unsafe places, a long ball and chain behind me.

I did not look directly at that ball and chain until later. After a while, the pattern of my penance became more obvious. Then, in my dreams and daydreams, an internal character emerged. I was not becoming psychotic—all of us have acknowledged or hidden aspects of ourselves that find reflection in movies and books, and expression in creative work and those wild nights when we act like "somebody else." I explored this character more directly. This method is arguably healthier, but such direct interest in fantasy may be one of the several reasons people find psychiatrists and psychologists to be "crazy."

This internal character was a profane and angry sort, loud and enraged for being padlocked in my psyche, far from my daily thoughts and behavior. He seemed uncouth and violent, not unlike some of the subjects of this book. I was horrified, perhaps explaining the padlocks. But when I examined this aspect of myself more closely, I could see that "he" was the part that could see right through dishonesty and mock respect. I had always found myself giving coworkers the benefit of the doubt, leading me to conclude that when someone was not the subject of forensic evaluation or study, I could be a bit gullible. Letting this seemingly dangerous part of me loose sharpened my sensibility and did not lead to violence.

I believe that all of us have dark, unexplained corners. We tend to vilify and extrude those that remind us of these aspects of ourselves. It is indeed like the horror movies—we burn the witch, hang the demon, and they come back again.

These observations are not meant to forgive killing. There is a thin but fundamental line between fantasy and action. All of us fantasize about murder. Most of us have muttered, "I'll kill you" aloud or under our breath more than once. Many repetitively enjoy murder mysteries and films. But our subsequent failure to acknowledge the similarity between ourselves and those who cross the line may backfire. Our strong but mixed feelings about murderers may make it difficult for us to allow those who should take responsibility for homicide to do so. I have traveled through the lives of murderers, and into the darker side of myself and those around me. I began my work with these men and women as an academic project as an associate of Harvard Medical School. Full of the diffidence of academics, I began with a supposition of murderers as the subjects of study, inmates, patients, distant beings whose awful lives had led them to kill. I was separate, an educated onlooker, taking notes and mumbling, "Hmm." Yet as I became involved in evaluation for the courts and treatment, my hands became dirty. In working many hours with them, I came to know murderers as fallible and tragic men and women. The crimes were no less wrong, but on closer approach, I became quite a bit more frightened knowing how thin the mask is that covers the murderer inside each of us. I also became more humble knowing how little difference there was between us. We place such awesome distances between ourselves as we arrange ourselves in endless intersecting hierarchies, hoping that we will wind up at the top of some. The humanity of the condemned called into question the purity of the exalted. Nonetheless, finding humanity in the barren confines of a prison gave me an odd hope. Perhaps the solution is not in cutting out the hearts of the murderers but in cultivating their ability to find their hearts and feel for others, and our ability to recognize ourselves in them.

23

Behind the Couch

UNDER THE LIGHT of the logic of patients, or under the glare of cross-examination, my journey brought the confusing intersection of psychiatry and law into full view for me. At first, as a new recruit to psychiatry, I blamed it all (or mostly) on the "other side." The law seemed rigid and simplistic. The discourse of the judges and lawyers seemed circuitous, if not dishonest. Each case was presented as the obvious conclusion of a studious review of previous cases. But as I became studious enough myself to know some of the cases, I saw that their conclusions were twisted to support outcomes desired for other reasons.

Still, the legal side forced me to explain, and thus examine, psychiatry. I did not always like what I found.

When I worked with psychiatrists untrained in legal matters, I often pointed out the legal implications of clinical issues. This translation was valued but not always what they wanted to hear. At those moments, I was not quite a "real" psychiatrist, but almost a bit of an attorney. Those moments of being neither in one camp nor the other gave me an ability to see both.

Psychiatry, at its best, is wonderful. It can help people see into the murky depths of the psyche and come out stronger, even healed. It is neither as fast nor as decisive as surgery, yet it is a powerful science, one that has vastly benefited from the arts, humanities, philosophy, and even mysticism. But like all powerful and mysterious arts, it has been the subject of intense scrutiny, criticism, and derision. The response has been revision and rebirth, but often at the expense of previous learning.

237

As I was being trained, psychoanalysis as the major basis of psychiatric understanding was already in the later stages of being toppled by biological psychiatry, and by trends beyond it. As I mentioned before, much of American psychiatry (less so in Europe) had been dominated by psychoanalytic theory for several decades. The peak of the influence of psychoanalysis may have been the 1950s. Many things may have contributed to this situation. Psychiatry was enjoying what many consider to be its greatest level of public esteem just after the war, due in part to the treatment of soldiers with shell shock (what we now call posttraumatic stress disorder). The nation was prosperous and saw itself as the leader of the Free World. New developments in science and technology seemed almost magical, barely behind the imagination of science fiction. Yet there was the threat of nuclear war, of a sudden invasion of a massively destructive force into a country that had seen no battles on the land since the American Civil War.

Perhaps the outer prosperity and the inner, dark fear (which erupted into the communist witch-hunt) was resonant with the themes of the conscious and unconscious mind—the power of unseen impulses usually seen as sexual. The psychoanalytic technique involved a "blank screen," the absence of extraneous chatter or displays of emotion by the therapist in order to let the patient project his or her unconscious images onto the therapist. Nonetheless, in more public communication, some analysts made rather wild claims regarding hopes of curing humankind.

The 1950s saw the introduction of chlorpromazine, the first major medication for psychosis. Institutional psychiatry slowly became more based on medication. Motivated by a humanitarian idealism, a community psychiatry movement in the 1960s advocated deinstitutionalization, leading in part to more homelessness for mentally ill people.

This deinstitutionalization was also caused by a more zealous movement that may have peaked in the late 1960s and 1970s. What some have called the antipsychiatry movement was fueled by the political and social upheaval of the time. R. D. Laing and Thomas Szasz were prominent leaders. This movement saw psychiatry as a means of social, and especially governmental, control. Some believed that mental illness was a myth, a label that enabled the government to isolate and chemically alter the minds of those who thought and behaved differently. Perhaps a bit more congenial and more compelling argument was that illness was an artifact of the societal system itself. The idea that the society then sought to hide away those afflicted by the system offered an intellectually attractive parallel to the issues of pollution and corruption. The movement rapidly moved from theory to action, leading to the passage of laws that made it difficult to place a person in a hospital and even harder to treat them if they voiced disagreement. These laws often allow obviously ill patients to languish in homelessness or in hospitals without medication. Ironically, a firebrand revolutionary (if he or she is threatening violence and appears to be mentally ill) is probably now easier to commit to a hospital than a person with schizophrenia who is quite ill but not violent. In essence, the legal bureaucracy took far-reaching control of the medical system. What started out as revolutionary became red tape. At roughly the same time, there was a movement to call patients clients. The rhetoric was about respect, but the term is borrowed from attorneys.

The term is now switching to consumers, and the practitioners are being called providers. With no loss of legal encumbrance, the business world is now taking over in the United States. The stated reason for these changes is the increasing cost of health care, but inside them is a larger revision, a rationing to meet business needs.

Along with the trends toward legal and business control, psychiatry has increasingly become oriented toward biology and medicine, and away from psychotherapy and psychoanalysis. This trend was disconcerting to me because I found that medication is important but no substitute for psychotherapy. Comparisons are difficult because each case is different, but, in general, although medication may be more powerful in the short term, psychotherapy can be more sustaining. Medication often works quickly to ameliorate symptoms. This apparent effectiveness may have a price. In patients with relatively minor illness but major life decisions, medication seems to challenge the status quo less than therapy.

I believe that psychiatric illness has meaning. For patients with serious illness, medication is often necessary to even begin to look at the deep issues in their lives. But for patients with less severe symptoms, medication can sometimes be used to "jump over" the meaning and relieve the symptom. It can allow the patient to then look at meaning either alone or in therapy, or avoid it. I believe in the use of medication but have had problems with the biological theory of behavior. At one point, I felt that biological theory's supplanting of psychotherapeutic ideas was a step backward in terms of the history of ideas. I now have hopes for a theory that incorporates the better aspects of both.

In the meantime, psychotherapy has continued to decline not only as a theory but also as a practice within psychiatry. The business forces seem to be decidedly antitherapy. Again, the rhetoric is financial—it is expensive, especially when done by physicians. The real reason, in my opinion, is more pernicious. Business tends to foster obedience and productivity. Independent thinking and creativity are valued, but usually in limited doses. Perhaps especially when a corporation reaches a large or dominant state, it values stability over change. Psychotherapy, especially in deeper forms, tends to promote change and development. I believe that much of the business world (erroneously and subconsciously) fears this change. Changing this aspect of corporations may be important not only for the psychotherapy of their employees, but also for there to be a switch to a focus on sustainable development, environmental balance, and cultural preservation in business.

So where does all of this leave murderers? There is an emerging set of biological hypotheses about violence. There are psychoanalytically based theories, but the literature is not as strong as it is in other areas. Even though violent fantasies are universal, thus providing a wealth of material for psychoanalytic scrutiny, murderers are unlikely to be in psychoanalysis.

There are other people who do the type of evaluations and work discussed here, and some of them do brilliant work. But there are a lot of gaps in theory, in practice, in understanding.

Sometimes, the cacophony of the legal arguments and the psychiatric viewpoints faded to silence. I was left sitting alone with someone who had killed, trying to figure out what I thought and then trying to find words for these thoughts in a language I no longer knew how to speak.

24

A Crisis of
Conscience

MY DIFFICULTIES with psychiatry and law led me to some tough questions. The idea of social control was particularly vexing. I dismissed it for a while because the idea seemed silly at its extreme. Mental illness was socially defined, and too flexible in some ways, although negating the concept was counterintuitive. But that was before I examined myself on a deeper level, along with whom I worked for, and what I represented. The legal system wants yes or no answers to vague questions. Being asked to distill a simple answer from a murky truth leads to enormous variability in interpretation. Some of the differences are theoretical—some psychiatrists have strong opinions that their colleagues don't share. It is difficult to make it clear that yours is a minority opinion if you think that you are right.

But there are other issues to weigh. Is it acceptable to consider the census requirements of a hospital in deciding whether someone is insane? The law says no, but such concerns often enter into the debate. Is it okay to consider how easy the person will be to treat? The law and psychiatry say no, but such issues inevitability color conclusions. Mental illness is socially defined, and so is its legal counterpart, insanity. That flexibility for practical concerns nagged at me. I wanted my evaluations to reach for a higher truth, but I was not sure that they did.

The struggles of a colleague helped me to understand these issues more deeply. She is a psychologist who was asked by the rest of the treatment team working with a patient to aid in pursuing his prosecution.

The patient had kicked several staff members and patients. Some had filed charges. Prosecuting patients in a hospital is controversial. Some people believe that the risk of violence in a psychiatric facility is part of the work. Others believe that some patients are not so much ill as evil, and they belong in prison. The latter was the sentiment of the staff in this case. Afraid and weary, they saw prison as an out (for them). Most of the staff had never been inside a prison—it was an idea, not an experience. When the psychologist consulted with me, I shared her ambivalence. Prison was someplace I knew. The hospital and staff would be safer if the patient moved, but was it best for the patient? Is prison good for anyone?

The conversation regarding this particular patient quickly turned to the specific legal issues at hand. The specific questions were easier to answer. The deeper issue of prison stayed with me.

It is obvious that most psychiatric evaluations related to criminal matters involve prison. If the person is fit to stand trial, not insane, and found to be guilty of a serious charge, then he or she is sentenced to prison. Psychiatrists are not asked about guilt and only about sentencing in a fairly indirect way (and rarely, in the settings where I have worked).

But prison looms. If the answer to an imperfect question is no and that of another murky question is yes, the person probably will go to prison. Of course, it is not the psychiatrist's direct choice or sentence.

That degree of separation was enough for me for a long time. But after a while, it bothered me. I wasn't sure exactly what was upsetting me at first. Often, understanding for me comes first visually, as pictures. Words follow. The picture that helped me in this regard is unpleasant but illustrative. I imagined that I was eating lunch and there was something inedible in my food. It doesn't matter what. I decided to eat around it.

Then, there was something else inedible. I decided to eat around it. I made the same decision once or twice more, until it became obvious that the problem wasn't something I could eat around.

I knew then that the prison issue was intrinsic to these evaluations, and that I had tried to avoid it, thinking that my work was separate and "clean" of it. It wasn't. That led to the next question: What was my problem with prison? I knew that I did not like any prison that I saw. I felt sad that many of the officers seemed as disillusioned as the prisoners. I thought it remarkable that some prisoners found spirituality, art, a new direction in prison; it seemed that they were the exception.

My thoughts returned me to an academic paper I had written earlier in my journey. In it, I had contrasted the correctional concepts of rehabilitation and punishment with the clinical goal of therapeutic care. I thought that punishment was especially incompatible with recovery. My conclusion encouraged fellow clinicians not to lose the goal of improvement. The paper and conclusion were reasonable enough, but on my return to the issues, it felt like "Eat around it."

I began to think more about the concept of punishment, even brood about it. We have had many phrases and ideas: "an eye for an eye," "cruel and unusual," "let the punishment fit the crime." The last one really rang in my head. I had other work to do, and I completed my tasks. But the issue of prison, of punishment, and that phrase kept coming up. Punishment fitting the crime. I realized slowly that the idea made no sense. I had a significant amount of training and knowledge in human behavior, crime, and law. But I did not know what punishment would fit what crime. It felt like I never would.

Finally, as this realization percolated, I asked, "Isn't punishment a crime?" I recalled the furor in the

United States when a young American was caned in Southeast Asia for what would be a minor crime at home. Yet building more prisons and capital punishment were becoming more popular.

Opposition to the death penalty is common in forensic psychiatry. Many forensic experts refuse to perform evaluations related to it; others, only if they are supplying information that may allow the person to avoid death. Few will conduct the evaluations entitled competency to be executed—a strange concept that holds that a person has to be in his or her "right mind" to be killed. This bizarre idea means that prisoners are sometimes medicated to regain mental capacity to then be killed. This particular evaluation has been the subject of great criticism from forensic psychiatry; it appears to be one of the most clear examples of the misuse (or abuse) of psychiatry by American state governments.

After all I had learned about the legal system and the limitations of psychiatry in helping it, I realized that I was opposed to more than the death penalty. I was opposed to punishment. I am not the first to voice such an opinion. But it surprised me that I had come to that point, and it left me with a strange feeling. I had found myself in a job that seemed in some ways acceptable, part of the society, sometimes even a bit routine. Suddenly, the edifice that supported it had collapsed and I did not know if I could do the job, if it was right, acceptable, or tolerable. I also was left with many other new questions.

The first was why did I think that punishment was wrong? Maybe I was not thinking straight, feeling burned out, tired, in need of a vacation. I could see the appeal of swift, accurate punishment. It had a decisive and symmetrical quality to it. But it perpetuates the suffering. We say murder is wrong, but it is legally acceptable for the state to kill. We say rape is wrong, but it is nearly condoned by prison systems and invoked in programs meant to scare people away from crime by pointing out how bad prison is.

Societies engaging in war embrace and promote violence and racism. Hitler's Germany was not the only culprit in this regard. The United States sequestered Japanese-Americans during the war, and all major combatants produced racist propaganda. One of the greatest problems in history has been what to do with the vigilant warrior, war-making mentality and machinery when the war is over. We train the warrior to be hard, cold, and unyielding, and then expect him or her to be kind when back home. Some of the soldiers in Vietnam coped by seeing war, literally, as hell. They saw the enemy as cruel and without honor. They saw the world they lived in the same way. Some adopted the credo they perceived around them; they became cruel and without honor too. The clash came when they returned and found that they were then supposed to behave normally and believe again in the society's honor. Some who returned before it was over began to see war and violence as the problem and opposed the war. It was a difficult position for a soldier to take. Others tried to assimilate back, but many had terrible problems believing in and integrating into the world they had left. Still others retained the view that they had during the war, and remained angry, suspicious, and cruel.

The military, in war, has used psychiatrists to assess who can return to the front and who receives a psychiatric discharge (which many soldiers have not wanted due to the stigma). Some armies have wanted the profession to "figure out" the enemy. Seen from the viewpoint of the war effort, such roles may seem appropriate. But they often run counter to the therapeutic goals of psychiatry. Saying that someone is fit enough to return to the front may be accurate, but many question whether it is therapeutic. These roles also may be the clearest examples of the use of the profession for social control.

Many believe that such military activities involve a suspension of normal rules, that the state has to take more power in time of war. Of course, the abuses of such power are well recorded. But how reasonable were the uses of power in peacetime, in the courts and prisons? I had observed firsthand that our criminal justice system is neither swift nor extremely accurate. The prisons are often cruel. It had become clear to me that the power to punish should be beyond (or perhaps better conceptualized as below) the powers of the state. Do we really want our governments, whose foibles and hidden agendas are legion, to mete out punishments? That idea, so commonplace and accepted, began to feel frightening, about as frightening as crime itself.

Crime, indeed, is the counterbalancing factor. We believe that punishment prevents crime. If the good guys don't do bad things to the bad guys, then the bad guys will win and do bad things to good people. There is often a pause, after the bad guy in the comic strip has done something rotten, before the superhero unleashes the fury. The pause is there to indicate "You made me do it." The fact that so many abusers of children utter the same words cannot escape notice.

There is a further parallel with abuse. There is often a parental aspect ascribed to nations—the motherland or fatherland. Governments have become very involved in the policing of parental abuse of children, generally becoming more vigilant and protective. Yet in the government's own handling of its sanctioned punishment of prisoners, it seems to be more and more lax. More punishing and, arguably, more abusive.

I came to the conclusion that the state was overstepping its bounds by inflicting punishment. But that left me with a big problem. If I had, in my imagination, eliminated prison and punishment, what should go in its place?

I would advocate a new system focusing on responsibility, choices, and restitution by the offender to the victim. Restitution is not new. Some scholars believe that the biblical phrase, "an eye for an eye," really meant restitution, not an equal corporal sacrifice. In feudal society, crime was punished by payment. The idea of restitution is very popular these days, but it is an add-on to a system of punishment. If we start to imagine restitution as the core of a new system, then that system starts to look very different. Instead of serving a few days in a crowded jail, the practitioner of a "minor" crime would have to come up with a plan of how he or she will not only live in a manner such as not to repeat the crime, but also provide restitution to the victim and the community. This suggestion does not mean that a wealthy criminal should pay off everyone. Earlier, I mentioned a neighborhood where I used to live, a place where the drug dealers ruled. In the middle of the neighborhood, surrounded by the open drug dealing, there was a little park, decrepit and run down. A small, modern, and misplaced sculpture stood in the corner of the park, so overwritten with graffiti that no messages were legible. Restitution for that neighborhood might mean that the convicted dealers should go out there and clean up the park, and perhaps replace that sculpture with one that had meaning for the community. These acts of restitution would not be intended to shame the dealers so much as to transform them, and to change their image in a neighborhood full of younger children who idolized them. Supervision would be necessary and perhaps costly.

Obviously, community-based interventions would not be enough. Society is coping clumsily with the fact that sexual offenders' sentences expire by trying to keep them under some kind of guard, sometimes by labeling them mentally ill. Sexual offenders or repetitively violent offenders might need isolation. It could be argued that a highly structured and supervised community program might be less costly and more productive in the long run. Megan's Law, if it is able to be followed fully, provides people with information about the sex offenders in their community. But it does not demand that treatment be available or that the offender use it. Megan Kanka's parents have said that their daughter's murder by a cognitively impaired man with a history of sexual offenses would not have occurred had they known the man's history. Perhaps that observation is true in their case, but I remain concerned that parental vigilance and possible overprotection might be difficult for parents and children, and arguably impossible in more crowded communities. A day program or residential treatment facility also might be preventive in some such situations.

How would the isolation program that I am suggesting be any different from prison? It would still need to be secure. But I believe that isolation can occur without punishment. Those in isolation could work to repay the victim and the community, perhaps learning a more productive role, and the effects of their previous actions, in the process. I strongly believe that these people should have to work for the community and to pay their way. I am not favoring a return to chain gangs, but claiming that prisoners must be paid to preserve their rights is a ridiculous misapplication of mercy. Treatment of mental disorders and substance abuse should play a more central role and may be more possible if offenders are not placed in prison. The current obsession with security can be kept to the perimeter of the facility. Inside, control would be maintained, but humanely. I see a group such as a parole board becoming involved early on, tracking the person's progress and determining what actions might be necessary next. Rather than being subjected to the current system of sentences and disciplinary actions, those in this system would have myriad choices to offer restitution. The choices would be determined by the nature of their crime, and by their behavior. So a person could be isolated further, kept away from others for a time if his or her behavior demanded it. But isolation would not be used as punishment.

Perhaps this proposal sounds like a semantic exercise, where *isolation* is another word for prison, and *discipline* is called a choice. Indeed, I fear that such could happen if there were moves to adopt a plan like this. The subtle but profound issue, however, is punishment itself. The system will fail if we ask it to exact revenge, because revenge is punishment. But if we decide that a person who commits a crime is to repay the community and the victim, and to reorganize his or her life, then we have the potential for a very different system.

There are many questions that arise when one proposes such major changes. Perhaps the most compelling is the most germane to this book. How can anyone repay for a life taken? Indeed, restitution for murder is perhaps absurd. The restitution can never equal the loss. Many families of the victims would not want to receive any restitution, even indirectly, from a person who killed a family member. Perhaps no one can adequately resolve these issues, although it is worthwhile to note that prison does not really address them either.

In my work with people who have killed, I have seen ways in which they could offer restitution, in a form that would not have to involve the victim's family. People who killed while on drugs should demonstrate more than abstinence; they should be active in the prevention of drug use. Previously violent people who have improved can help to prevent violence by teaching others—not so much to scare them, but wake them up. I can imagine a group of ex-convicts making a film about the changes in your life after you hurt someone. The film could be an alternative to the glamorization of violence in the media. None of these activities makes up for a life lost but might have a positive impact on the community.

I believe there should be a financial side to the restitution as well. People who have killed should attempt to pay for their treatment, isolation, and restitution to the victim or community. The work, whenever possible, would be rehabilitative.

Release from isolation, or any secure facility, would occur in small, graduated steps, so that the person can be watched closely as he or she nears reentry into the community. Some people may need more time than others, which would be determined not only by the nature of the crime but also by their progress. The payment no longer is time; it is restitution.

Perhaps most important, abuse has to be eliminated: both the abuse by the current prisoners and guards. It will be a long road, but the state psychiatric hospitals have faced similar, if less severe, issues with some success.

Wouldn't sociopaths just wriggle through a system like the one I described? Indeed, they may attempt to fool any new system by feigning improvement to be freed. Some researchers have suggested that group therapy with sociopaths may actually help, perhaps because they do not fool each other. The early identification of effective sociopaths may be the key to prevention of falsehood; it is theoretically possible that a group approach might help in terms of monitoring. Addressing the long-term concerns regarding sociopaths and sex offenders, it seems likely that the small steps into the community would need to include a broad array of ways of monitoring the behavior of previous criminals in the community. While some advocates (and criminals) might actually prefer the all-or-nothing aspect of prison and release, a well-run set of community programs might maximize freedom while also improving overall safety, since there would likely be lower costs and therefore less pressure to release prematurely.

If a repeat offense including murder means that the program has failed, then it will fail. There is no perfect program. Most attempts at innovation regarding prison are shut down when someone from the program commits another crime. The publicity of one brutal offense is often enough to close a program and lead to cries for more prisons. That result seems logical enough, but the solution is always more prison, something that we know does not prevent repeat crimes after release. Only a realistic comparison with prison can determine the effectiveness of another concept. No program except death or life imprisonment completely prevents repeat crimes, and those are extreme and costly measures.

When I first started thinking about these changes, I feared that I was bizarre. There is a lot of talk about community programs and gradual steps to release, but few are talking about abolishing prisons. Yet, the more I pondered prisons, the more they seemed barbaric. I can easily imagine a child of the future aghast that such an abusive system lasted for so long.

I realized how deeply prison affected my work, that I could no longer think that my evaluations were separate and apart from it. I think that many psychiatrists and psychologists struggle with this issue. In one locality that I know of, this concern has led to evaluators deeming many defendants insane that probably are not. If a case can be made, they may err far on the side of favoring someone going to a hospital rather than a prison. While this is understandable, the sad result is that the hospital there is clogged, and people who need to be hospitalized wind up getting arrested since they can't get in. Some of these very ill people probably wind up in prison, so the net effect may be negative.

I finally realized that I can no longer do the kind of evaluations that involve prison. That may seem like an easy decision, but it was not. Some of the other people who do such evaluations are not skilled or trained to do them. Some friends and colleagues feel that the system needs people who struggle with the issues, that by my opting out, the people get less service, not more. But, the idea of prison and state punishment seems so absurd to me that it taints all of the work. All of the questions, and all of the answers that I can formulate, seem moot in the face of that absurdity.

I will continue to work in the crossroads between psychiatry and the law. My work with murderers, other defendants, and patients has prepared me to examine another area of forensic psychiatry. Some of the issues I found that affected many of the patients are the province of civil rather than criminal law. Many of the female patients have been victims of frank abuse and subtler forms of sexist treatment. Ethnic and racial discrimination are also often underreported. There is a need for a closer look at these issues regarding patients and others.

My departure from criminal forensic psychiatry was one important reason why I left work at a clinical, research, and teaching position with a state hospital and university. It was harder to leave the patients I treated there than it was to leave the idea of the work itself. The departure from that job seemed simple at first, but I realized it was more symbolic. I could no longer work within the criminal legal system, but I also have spiritually divorced myself from much of current psychiatric theory. The uncertainties and questions that I had discovered are important, and unresolved. I began to design a series of research projects to address these issues, to attempt to understand the theoretical gaps that are present not only in psychiatry but also in medicine and science at large. As long as these gaps remain unbridged, they will prevent us from adequately addressing the issues of culture, gender, and our own biases that bear so much responsibility for our social ills, as seen in many of the patients' stories documented here. It is an unfortunate indication of the status quo that my inquiries have encountered strong and immediate objection. Challenging accepted thought and methodology always draws opposition, but in science, open-mindedness should be the norm. Although sometimes personally difficult to deal with, the objections that I have had to overcome have strengthened my resolve to pursue this area of research; they have underscored the importance of the work.

I now realize that when I started my career, I believed many partial truths as gospel and accepted the biases of the moment. Disappointment and disillusionment with the system and the ideas that form its philosophical foundation were the impetus to my departure. It started at the level of theory and progressed to a move from the setting of a large university and hospital to a small organization. These changes have facilitated a constantly unfolding journey forward and inward, a search to find a quieter, more personal, and yet universal solution to the problems within psychiatry and related fields.

So in a way that I never imagined at the beginning, the journey ends. I leave my work with murderers not out of fear of them or even of their likeness within me. I leave because I cannot represent the cruelty of a system that I worked for, a system that systematically and regularly hurts people in the name of justice.

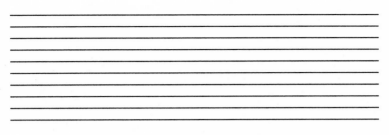

Acknowledgments

I FIRST MUST acknowledge the learning I gathered from my work with patients, defendants, and inmates at various institutions. I also learned much about the real story behind the obvious from the staff. My mentors in forensic psychiatry continue to be great sources of information, although I take full responsibility for any inaccuracies in this book. Thomas Gutheil, M.D., taught me not only the facts but also how to think like a researcher and scholar. Seymour Halleck, M.D., nurtured my excitement about the topic and helped me along the way. James Gilligan, M.D., and Shervert Frazier, M.D, looked over my shoulder in my forensic training and made it all seem fascinating and somehow fathomable. Roderick Pettis, J.D., M.D., supported and challenged my ideas in numerous sessions. He and Opal Thornton, M.D., Ken Galen, M.D., Marcus Goldman, M.D., James Reinhard, M.D., Emily Keram, M.D., and Steve Keram, J.D., M.D., exchanged ideas and shared our experiences learning to be members of an unusual guild. Other psychiatry mentors include Salman Akhtar, M.D., Jeffry Andresen, M.D., Robert Golden, M.D., Dwight Evans, M.D., Jarrett Barnhill, M.D., John McDermott, M.D., Naleen Andrade, M.D., and J.C. Garbutt, M.D. Colleagues and friends who helped my growth include Jim Edwards, M.D., Suzanne Witterholt, M.D., Harry Goldwasser, M.D., Maeveen Behan, J.D., Beverly Redmann, M.D., John Wise, Kenneth Chavin, M.D., Ph.D., I. Favel Chavin, M.D., Andrew Leamy, Richard Kingsley, M.D., Gregory Sazima, M.D., Scott Sazima, D.D.S., Thomas Falkenberg, M.D.,

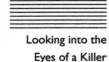
and the coinventor of a powerful form of deviated theory, Vince Eoppolo.

People who helped me to write the book include Harry and Rose Rudnick, Rose Ross, Phyllis and Donald Ross, Brandon Ross, Doug Ross, Karen and Dave McKenica, and Aleen Grabow, M.D. Stephen Dixon always believed in my writing. Laine Jenkins, M.D., was a tremendous support early in the process. The book would not be finished without the reading, editing, and nudging of Terri Klein. The editor of the book, Erika Goldman, was an enthusiastic supporter, and Diana Finch was the agent who helped to shape the structure of the book and to find a publisher. Catherine Burton, Ph.D., Judith Orodenker, and Stuart Silverman, M.D., helped me realize and work through the crisis of conscience. Stefani Scotto reminded me for and with whom I really write.

Index

Adolescents
  as gang members, 208–210
  as murderers, case study of,
      168–171
  sexual abuse of, 92
  violent fantasies of, 169
African Americans, as gang
      members, 208–210
Aggression
  prevalence of, 125–126
  sublimation of, 68
Alcoholics Anonymous (AA), 21
Alcohol use
  as disinhibition cause, 11, 114
  as drunk driving cause, 26–27
  as murder risk factor, 11
American Psychiatric Associa-
      tion, 159
Antipsychiatry movement, 239
Antisocial behavior
  paternal factors in, 226
  society's acceptance of,
      157–160
Antisocial personality disorder,
      case studies of, 157–159
Armored car robber, case study
      of, 71–79
Arson, 157, 158–159
Asia, 34, 35, 247–248
Assassination attempts, 38–39
Assaults
  disinhibition-related, 113–117
  on hospital patients, 165
  by prison inmates, 123, 168
Attica prison, 122

Bedlam, 38
Behavior, biological theory of,
      240
Beliefs, delusional: see Delu-
      sional beliefs
Biological theory
  of behavior, 240
  of criminal behavior, 41–42, 43
  of psychological disorders,
      42–43, 238
  of violence, 24
Bipolar disorder: see Manic-
      depression
Blame
  externalization of, 27
  grief-related, 218
"Blank screen" technique, of psy-
      choanalysis, 238
Borderline personality disorder,
      32–33
Brain injuries, relationship to
      criminal behavior, 42, 43,
      114
Bribery, emotional, 24–25
Bureaucracy, in mental health
      care, 189–190

Caning, 247–248
Capital punishment, 248
Child abuse, 43
  government's response to,
      250
  memories of, 203–204
  of murderers, case studies of,
      109–110, 130, 131

Childhood
experience of violence during, 223–225
memories of, 202–203, 204
Childlike behavior, psychotic, 201–204
Children
abused: *see* Child abuse
hyperactivity syndrome of, 42
inner-city, life expectancy of, 210
Chinese medicine, 35
Chlorpromazine, 238
Civil commitment, 34–35
Clinical improvement, as psychiatric goal, 11–12, 247
Cognitive disability of murderers, case studies of, 109–117
Cognitive processing, effect of psychosis on, 168
Cognitive psychotherapy, 32–33
Cold War, 10, 238
Common law, English, 34
Community-based interventions, for criminal offenders, 251–252, 254–255
Confidentiality, of therapist–patient relationship, 75–77
Corporations
antisocial behavior in, 157–160
psychotherapy use in, 240–241
Correctional officers
boredom experienced by, 122
inappropriate behavior of, 115–117
job responsibilities of, 122
motivations of, 231
profanity use by, 115–116
relationship with prisoners
emotional and verbal abuse, 115–116, 146, 147
example of, 121–124
unwritten code of conduct for, 116, 122
Crime, unsolved, patients' confession of, 76

Criminal behavior
biological basis of, 41–42, 43
motivations for, 41, 74
psychotic criminals' memory of, 167–168
Criminally insane, 32
Criminals, with mental illness
psychiatric evaluation of: *see* Psychiatric evaluations
treatment approaches to, 32
prior to trial, 40

Dangerousness, determination of, 37–38
Death, murderers' fascination with, 11
Defense projection, 172
Deinstitutionalization, 110–111, 238–239
Delusional beliefs, 132–134
case studies of, 134–140, 187–190
of manic-depressive patients, 187–190
thought patterns associated with, 134
Dependency, in therapist–patient relationship, 178
Depression, case studies of, 43–45
Desensitization, 175–176, 238–239
Developmentally-disabled patients, institutionalization of, 110–111
Diagnostic process, 165–166
Discipline, in prisons, 116, 148, 253
Disinhibition, 113–117
Doing/undoing, 33
Drug abuse
as brain injury cause, 42
by criminals with mental illness, 32
maternal, 91
by murderers, 11
case studies of, 21–22, 23–24, 91, 92, 93, 215–217, 218–219
restitution for, 253

Drug dealing, in prison, 151–153, 168
Drug therapy
disadvantages of, 240
as murder defense, 217
patients' opposition to, 196–197
psychotherapy versus, 240
relationship to capital punishment, 248
for schizophrenia, 181–182
Drummond, Edward, 39

Eisenhower, Dwight, 208
Emotion
physical basis of, 35
sociopaths' feigning of, case studies of, 24–25, 151–153
Emotional abuse, by correctional officers, 116–117
Expert witnesses, 33, 40, 55
Externalization, 27

Fantasies
grief-related, 218
"marionette," 129, 132
psychiatrists' interest in, 232
relationship to reality, 106
rescue, 138
violent, 241
of adolescents, 169
about murder, 101–106, 230, 232–233
sexual, 111–112, 115
Farming, mental patients' involvement in, 50–51
Fatal Attraction (film), 32
Fathers, influence on sons' antisocial behavior, 226
Fear, *see also* Paranoia
as motivation for murder, 176–181
Ferrers, Earl, 3
Fights, 42
among children, 223–225, 231
Flirting, 68

Forensic psychiatrists
desensitization of, 175–176, 229–230
motivations of, 52–57, 225–233
opposition to capital punishment, 248
racial bias of, 171–172
rescue fantasies of, 138
responsibility of, 32
safety concerns of, 124–125
voyeurism experienced by, 226–229
Forensic psychiatry, 31–32, 33
Freud, Sigmund, 31, 33, 36–37, 42–43

Gangs, 169–171, 207–210
Greeks, ancient, 33–34
Grief, 218

Harvard Medical School, 233
Head injuries: *see* Brain injuries
Hinckley, John, 39
Hitler, Adolf, 249
Homelessness, of the mentally ill, 238, 239
Homophobia, of paranoid patient, 94–95
Honor
of gangs, 207
in war, 249
Hospitalization
civil commitment process for, 34–35
of criminal patients, 34–35
psychiatric evaluations for: *see* Psychiatric evaluations
Hospitals
prosecution of patients in, 246
state psychiatric
admission process of, forensic psychiatrist's experience of, 53–56
farms associated with, 51
violence against patients in, 165
Human nature, inherent goodness versus evil of, 50
Hyperactivity, 42

Impulse, irresistible, *see also* Dis-
    inhibition
  as insanity defense standard,
    129
Impulse control, lack of: *see* Dis-
    inhibition
Incest, 63, 64, 84, 86, 193–195
Indigenous cultures, 50
Infanticide, case study of,
    215–219
Insanity, statutory definition of,
    139, 171
Insanity defense, 12–13
  historical background of, 38–39
  legal system's attitude to-
    wards, 12–14
  M'Naghten rule for, 39
  multiple personality disorder
    as basis for, 129–130
  psychiatric evaluation for:
    see Psychiatric evalua-
    tions
  standards for, 39, 129
Insanity evaluations: *see* Psychi-
    atric evaluations
Institutionalization, of
    developmentally-disabled
    persons, 110–111
Intelligence, of psychotic per-
    sons, 132
Internal characters, 231–232
Intimacy
  paranoid patients' desire for,
    94–95, 97–98
  paranoid patients' fear of, 95,
    180, 181

Janet, Pierre, 36
Japanese-Americans, World War
    II internment of, 249
Jealousy, as motivation for mur-
    der, 83–87
Jung, Carl, 33
Jungian theory, 33, 66
Justice, 34

Kanka, Megan, 252
Kohut, Heinz, 139
Kraepelin, Emil, 36

Laing, R.D., 239
Laws, relationship to human be-
    havior, 195–196
Legal system
  adversarial nature of, 33–34
  attitudes towards insanity de-
    fense, 12–14
  borderline personality disorder
    analogy of, 32–33
  "legal time" aspect of, 195
  non-ambivalence of, 32–33
  relationship to psychiatry,
    32–45, 237, 245–255
  punishment issue, 247–249,
    250
  social control issue, 245
  religious and moral basis of,
    33–34
Lifestyle, simple, 50–51
Logic, binary, 33
Lying, by sociopaths, 25

Manic-depression
  case studies of, 187–190
  early research about, 36
"Marionette fantasy," of mental
    illness, 129, 132
Marxist theory, 159
Media, *see also* Television
  coverage of murders by, 9, 49
  depiction of murderers by, 176
Medication use, *see also* Drug
    therapy
  as murder defense, 217
Megan's Law, 252
Memories
  of childhood, 202–203, 204
  of childhood abuse, 203–204
  illusory capabilities of, 202–203
Mental health care, bureaucracy
    in, 189–190
Mental illness
  multifactorial etiology of,
    43–45
  as myth, 239
Mental retardation, case study
    of, 113–117
Metal detectors, use in prisons,
    144

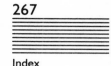

M'Naghten, Daniel, 39
M'Naghten rule, of insanity defense, 39
Monro, John, 38
Moral behavior, mental illness and, 133
Movie characters, identification with, 21, 229
Movies
    depiction of sadism in, 98
    depiction of violence in, 227–229
    produced by ex-convicts, 253–254
Multiple personality disorder, 129–130
Murder
    dreams and fantasies about, 101–106, 230, 232–233
    by gangs, 207
    of infant, case study of, 215–219
    as inherently insane act, 170
    media coverage of, 9, 49
    model of, 10–11
    of police officers, 135–136, 196–197
    predisposing factors in, 11
    premeditated, 11, 132
    prevention of, 49
    in prison, 168, 215
    public's fascination with, 49, 51, 56
    by stalker, case study of, 83–87
    universality of, 229
Murderers
    avoidance of, 51–52
    behavior in prison, 168
    denial by, 217
    empathy with, 232–233
    media's depiction of, 105–106, 176, 230
    public's fascination with, 56
    serial, case study of, 72–74, 76

Narcissism, 139
Narcotics Anonymous (NA), 21, 217
National Geographic, 130, 131

Neurochemical theory, of criminal behavior, 41–42
Neurologic illness, 32

Observable phenomena, 35–36
Obsessive behavior, 134
Oklahoma City, U.S. Federal Building bombing, 9–10
Organized behavior, case study of, 134–140
Oxford, Edward, 38–39

Paranoia, 94–95
    case studies of, 95–98, 134–140, 163–165, 175–183, 196–197
    fear associated with, 176–181
    of gang members, case study of, 209–210
    of prison cultures, 147
    schizophrenia-related, case study of, 181–182
Pearl Harbor, Japanese attack on, 10
Peel, Robert, 39
Physical abuse, 109–110
Physics, 36
Plato, 33–34
Plea bargains, 75
Police officers, murder of, 135–136, 196–197
Pornography, violence in, 227
Posttraumatic stress disorder, 238
Power structure, of prisons, 116, 122–124
Premeditated murder/premeditation, 11, 132
Prison(s)
    alternatives to, 250–255
    discipline in, 116, 148, 253
    forensic psychiatrist's reactions to, 143–148
    inmate–correctional officer relationship in, 115–116, 146, 147
    isolation from society, 143
    physical characteristics of, 143–145

Prison(s) (*cont.*)
  power structure of, 116,
    122–124
  psychiatric hospitalization ver-
    sus, 246
  punishment in, 148, 231
  rules in, 148
  security procedures in,
    143–144
  "snitching" behavior in, 116,
    146, 152
Prison culture, paranoia of, 147
Prisoners' rights movement, 148
Prison inmates
  isolation from society, 148
  "pecking order" among, 22
  relationship with correctional
    officers,
    emotional and verbal abuse,
      115–116, 146, 147
    example of, 121–124
  as repeat offenders, 228
Prison staff: *see* Correctional officers
Profanity, use in prisons,
  115–116
Prohibition, gangsters during,
  207–208
Psychiatric evaluations, 32,
  37–38, 246
  death penalty-related, 248
  paradox of, 170
  racism in, 171–172
  relationship to criminal inves-
    tigations, 74–76
Psychiatry, *see also* Forensic psychiatry
  ambivalence of, 33
  biological theory-based, 42–43,
    238
  clinical improvement goal,
    11–12, 247
  comparison with legal system,
    32–45, 237, 245–255
    punishment issue, 247–249,
      250
    social control issue, 245
  diagnostic approach of, 13–14
  empiricism of, 35–36

Psychiatry (*cont.*)
  inability to explain violent be-
    havior, 12
  military aspects of, 249–250
  misuse of, 248
  revisions of, 237–240
  scientific basis of, 35–36
  social movement against,
    239
  spiritual/mystical approach,
    35–36, 237
Psychoanalysis, 238, 240
Psychosis
  definition of, 171
  diagnosis of, racial factors in,
    171–172
  effect on cognitive processing,
    168
  neurochemical basis of, 201
  psychotic recession theory of,
    201–204
Psychosomatic disorders, 42
Psychotherapy, drug therapy versus, 240
Psychotic recession, 201–204
Psychopaths: *see* Sociopaths
Punishment
  correctional officers' desire for,
    231
  as crime, 247–249
  government's administration
    of, 250
  in prisons, 148, 231
  restitution as, 251

Quantum physics, 36

Racism
  in psychiatric evaluations,
    171–172
  during wartime, 249
  towards African-American
    gang members, 208
Rape
  of hospital patients, 165
  of prison inmates, 248–249
Rape victims
  public attitudes towards, 67
  rapists' blame of, 67–68

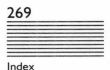

Rapists, case studies of, 61–68, 91–94
Rationality, differentiated from reality, 133
Ray, Isaac, 133
Reagan, Ronald, 39
Reality
  denial of, 176
  relationship to fantasy, 106
  relationship to rationality, 133
  subjectivity of, 202
Reductionist theory, of research, 166
Relativity, 36
Religious mania, 187–190
Remorse, 164–165, 167–168
  sociopaths' false expression of, 25
  subjectivity of, 170, 171
Renaissance, 36
Rescue fantasies, 138
Research, 166–167
  empiricism of, 167
  reductionist theory of, 166
  in therapist–patient relationship, 182
Responsibility, for criminal behavior, 41
Restitution, by criminal offenders, 251, 252–254
Rules, in prisons, 148

Sadism
  depiction in movies, 98
  of paranoid patients, 94
Schizophrenia
  case studies of, 181–182, 197
  drug therapy for, 181–182
  early research about, 36
  hospitalization for, 239
  "marionette fantasy" theory of, 129
  resistance to treatment of, 197
Scientific discovery, process of, 36–37
"Second thoughts," lack of: see Disinhibition

Self-multilation, 188
Sentencing, 246
Serial murderer, case study of, 72–74, 76
Sexual abuse, of adolescents, 92
Sexual abuse victims, as violence perpetrators, 92–93, 98
Sexual activity, in prison, 168
Sexuality, violent
  case studies of, 91–98, 109–117
  fantasies about, 111–112, 115
Sexual offenders, punishment of, 251–252
Shadow, The (radio program), 65
Shadow theory, 66–67
Shell shock, 238
Simpson, O.J., 9, 56
Skinner, B.F., 33
Snack food use, as murder defense, 217
"Snitching," in prisons, 116, 146, 152
Social conflict, 11
Social control, 245, 249–250, 245
Social isolation
  of criminal offenders, 251–253
  of paranoid patients, 95, 97
Social worker, murder of, by patient, 178–179
Socioeconomic status, relationship to antisocial personality behavior, 157–160
Sociopaths
  case examples of, 19–27
  characteristics of, 22–23, 25
Sodomy, 94
Soldiers, psychiatric discharge of, 249
Solitary confinement, 116, 143
Stabbings, by prison inmates, 123
Stalker, murder committed by, 83–87
Stress, 42–43
Support, lack of, as murder risk factor, 11
Szasz, Thomas, 239

Looking into the
Eyes of a Killer

Television
    depiction of murderers on,
        105–106
    depiction of violence on, 68
    as violence cause
        case studies of, 74, 77, 78–79
        in children, 77
        in socially-isolated individu-
            als, 77–79
Terrorism, 9–10
Testimony, psychiatric, see also
        Expert witnesses
    historical background of, 38–39
Theory, 140
    development of, in clinical set-
        ting, 167
Therapeutic bond, 165–166
Therapist, murder of, by patient,
        178–179
Therapist–patient relationship
    confidentiality of, 75–77
    dependency in, 178
    fear in, 176–181
    meaasurement of, 182
Thinking patterns
    "black-and-white," 32–33
    by borderline personality disor-
        der patients, 32–33
    fragmented/disorganized, 134
Threats
    against correctional officers, 124
    by correctional officers, 115

Truth, therapeutic, 203–204
Turner, Ike, 208

Unconscious, 36–37
United Kingdom, insanity de-
        fense in, 38–39, 129

Victoria, Queen, 38–39
Vietnam War, 249
Violence
    attitudes towards, 49–50
    biological theory of, 241
    childhood experience of, 43,
        223–225; see also Child
        abuse
    historical tradition of, 207–
        208
    in hospitals and psychiatric fa-
        cilities, 165, 246
    in pornography, 227
    random, 114–115
    sexual: see Sexuality, violent
    suppression of emotional reac-
        tions to, 176
    during war, 249
    in Western society, 50
Voyeurism, experienced by foren-
        sic psychiatrists,
        226–229

War, 249
Women, as sexual objects, 86–87

About the Author

DREW ROSS, M.D. is President of Alef Ani, a scientific research organization, and is Associate Clinical Professor of Psychiatry at the John A. Burns School of Medicine at the University of Hawaii. He has taught at Harvard Medical School and has received Honorable Mention from the Keyes Award in Psychiatry and from the Fellows Award of the American Academy of Forensic Sciences. A consulting editor at *The American Journal of Psychotherapy,* he has published numerous articles in professional journals.